Color

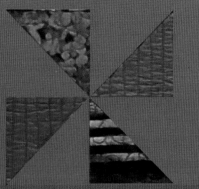

COLOR GETS ALL THE CREDIT IN A QUILT

When we see a quilt we like in a quilt show, on the wall of a quilt shop, or in a book, we often say to ourselves or to someone we are with, "Ooh, I love that quilt." We are usually referring to the colors in the quilt. We humans love color. We think quilts are great because of the colors. We look for fabrics to make a quilt we saw and loved—the *same* fabric, if possible, that the quilter used. Many of us are disappointed if we can't find that exact fabric.

COLOR WHEELS

A color wheel can be a great tool to use when planning your quilts. It is very easy to use. It's not just for artists: it is also for you and me—people who love quilts, and make quilts, and don't have an art background. Remember, no one is born knowing about color and which colors look good together. Everyone has to learn this skill. The good news is that it *is* learnable, and a color wheel is a great learning tool.

There are two kinds of color wheels widely available in quilt shops and/or art supply stores.

The traditional color wheel has been around for years. Color wheels with windows are newer. You can lay your fabric under the windows and see exactly where the fabric fits—what color it matches best.

I like both color wheels for different reasons. The traditional one has no windows, but all twelve colors (primary, secondary, and tertiary) are clearly and simply shown and labeled on the *front* of the color wheel.

The color wheel with windows has labels, too, but they are on the reverse side, so to identify the correct color family, you have to flip the color wheel over. To me, this color wheel is less clear for that reason. My color wheel like this one is bent on the edges. What I do love about this color wheel is the windows. It is so easy to see if a fabric is closer to blue or closer to blue-green or closer to blue-violet. (Then I bend the edges to make sure I'm right!)

hint

I found the windows especially helpful with quilts like *Triple Berry Tumble* and *Lemon Blueberry Pound Cake*. *Triple Berry Tumble* includes red-orange and blue-green. *Lemon Blueberry Pound Cake* features yellow-orange and blue-violet. Just as an example, blue-violet, often called periwinkle, is a difficult fabric to choose. Sometimes a blue-violet fabric looks bluer; other times it looks purple. Verify your choice using the color wheel with windows. This technique works well with any color but is especially helpful with colors like red-orange, yellow-orange, blue-green, and blue-violet—the colors used in *Triple Berry Tumble* and *Lemon Blueberry Pound Cake*.

COLOR TERMS
A Word about Primary, Secondary, and Tertiary Colors; Complementary Pairs; and Analogous Colors

In general, **primary colors** are colors from which other colors are made. We consider red, blue, and yellow to be primary colors. By combining these colors, the other colors on the color wheel are created.

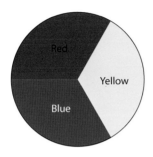

Primary Colors

Secondary colors are made by combining two primary colors. Red + yellow = orange. Yellow + blue = green. Blue + red = violet (purple). There are three secondary colors—orange, green, and violet (purple).

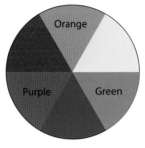

Secondary Colors

Tertiary colors are made by combining a primary and a secondary color. Red + orange = red-orange. Orange + yellow = yellow-orange. Yellow + green = yellow-green. Green + blue = blue-green. Blue + purple = blue-violet. Purple + red = red-violet. There are six tertiary colors. When you create tertiary colors, the primary color name is listed first. For example, *red-orange* is correct; *orange-red* is not.

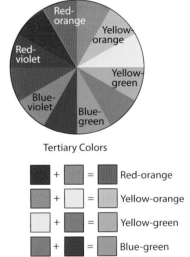

Tertiary Colors

■ + □ = ■ Red-orange
□ + □ = □ Yellow-orange
□ + ■ = ■ Yellow-green
■ + ■ = ■ Blue-green
■ + ■ = ■ Blue-violet
■ + ■ = ■ Red-violet

Complementary pairs are colors that are opposite on the color wheel. Because there are twelve colors on the color wheel (primary, secondary, and tertiary), there are many combinations!

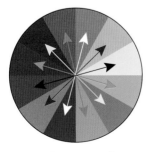

Complementary Colors

Complementary colors share a unique relationship. They always look good together. They "complement" and highlight each other. Possible complementary combinations using only primary and secondary colors are red and green, orange and blue, yellow and purple. Possible complementary combinations using tertiary colors are red-orange and blue-green (*Triple Berry Tumble Quilt*), yellow-orange and blue-violet (*Lemon Blueberry Pound Cake Quilt*), yellow-green and red-violet.

There you have it—six quilts are possible with just the above color combinations.

There are twelve possibilities if you do a single (monochromatic) quilt in each color family (an all-red quilt, for example). Remember that you can combine single colors with neutrals, such as black, white, cream, tan, or muslin. An all-red quilt could be red and black, or red and white, or red and cream/tan/muslin. Or an all-red quilt could be made with different values of red, such as pink and red. There are many possibilities with just one color!

SANDY BONSIB

Patchwork *Party*

10 Festive New Quilts & the Recipes That Inspired Them

C&T PUBLISHING

Text copyright © 2009 by Sandy Bonsib

Artwork copyright © 2009 by C&T Publishing, Inc.

Publisher: Amy Marson

Creative Director: Gailen Runge

Editor: Deb Rowden

Technical Editor: Georgie Gerl

Copyeditor/Proofreader: Wordfirm Inc.

Cover Designer: Christina D. Jarumay

Book Designer: Kerry Graham

Page Layout Artist: Publishers' Design and Production Services

Production Coordinators: Tim Manibusan and Casey Dukes

Illustrators: Kim Jackson and Mary Flynn

Photography by Christina Carty-Francis and Diane Pedersen of C&T Publishing, Inc., unless otherwise noted.

Published by C&T Publishing, Inc., P.O. Box 1456, Lafayette, CA 94549

Library of Congress Cataloging-in-Publication Data

Bonsib, Sandy

 Patchwork Party : 10 festive new quilts & the recipes that inspired them / Sandy Bonsib.

   p. cm.

 Summary: "10 pieced quilt projects paired with the recipes that inspired them"—Provided by publisher.

 ISBN 978-1-57120-624-4 (paper trade : alk. paper)

1. Patchwork--Patterns. 2. Desserts. 3. Desserts in art. I. Title.

 TT835.B628244 2009

 746.46'041--dc22

                              2008050939

Printed in China

10 9 8 7 6 5 4 3 2 1

Dedication

This book is dedicated to my web designer, Kim Jackson. She is an amazing person. For the last five years, she has created my dessert quilt patterns, all 23 of them, somehow figuring out my hieroglyphics, creating poor or lacking illustrations where they were needed, and fixing my bad quilt photographs so they look bright and attractive. Before that, she created my workshop handouts. And before that, she created my website. When she took that job on, she had never created a website before. I have received many compliments on my website over the years, and it has not significantly changed since Kim created it. Kim has also created my colorful business cards. The list goes on and on. Her attitude is amazing. She is always willing to help, to learn, and to try whatever I ask her to do. We have learned together, and it has been a wonderful journey. I couldn't do what I have done for the last ten years without her!

Acknowledgments

First, I thank my wonderful, supportive husband, John Bickley. After 29 years of marriage, he is still the nicest guy in the world. He is amazingly supportive in so many ways, and I really wouldn't have the time and energy to create books without his tireless help.

Thank you to my wonderful, loyal students. You have taught me so much and enriched my life and my teaching in unexpected ways. You have come to many classes, some of you to all or most of my classes about dessert quilts (which now number 23)! I consider you dear, loyal friends. In this book, the quilt titled *Valentine Cookies* is dedicated to you. The description of this quilt says it all: In my heart you are all stars. You make beautiful quilts, stretch my ideas, change my colors, and in general do very little that I tell you to do—so I learn so much from you, and I love you all.

Thank you to Carrie Peterson, who quilted all my quilts in this book and many of my students' quilts. Carrie does an amazing job. She works so hard to make sure each and every quilt is unique, and her design creativity is endless. She is also one of the nicest people I have ever known.

Thank you to Deb Rowden, my editor. It has been a pleasure to work with you from the day I met you. Thank you for all your hard work to make this book a great success.

Thank you to Georgie Gerl for being such an excellent technical editor. You are professional, creative, and very open to suggestions. You are so easy to work with.

Thank you to Kerry Graham. You are a very talented book designer. I asked for lots of color, and you used so much color and arranged the text in so many different, wonderful ways. Thank you so much for all the creativity you put into this book.

Thank you to Tim Manibusan and Casey Dukes for all your work coordinating everything in this book. I am very happy with how this book has come together, and I thank you both for all your time and effort.

And, finally, thank you to C&T Publishing for believing in me again. It has been a pleasure to work with you on another book. I hope this is just the beginning for us as a team.

CONTENTS

Introduction

Enjoy our latest patchwork quilts inspired by the rich colors of delicious desserts (following *Sweet Treats*).

Inside you will find ten new projects: pieced quilts paired with the recipes that inspired them.

Here's how this began: when I teach quilt classes locally, I take the matching dessert for my students to eat. Everyone then spends six hours sewing, chatting, and eating. It doesn't get much better than that!

Throughout the book you'll find luscious patchwork shared by my students too. Look for their work following each project and in the two quilt challenges: the It's a Mystery Challenge, on page 80, and the Lemon Chiffon Quilt Challenge, on page 82.

I never expected these quilts and desserts to evolve into one book, let alone two!

ENJOY!

Sandy

NOW LET'S PLAY AROUND

You don't have to look across the color wheel to find interesting combinations. You can combine colors that are next to each other on the color wheel. These are called **"analogous"** colors. You can use three or more analogous colors together. You can use only primary and secondary analogous colors, making a quilt that is blue, purple, and red. Or you can expand to tertiary colors and make a quilt that is blue, blue-violet, and purple. Add some more colors—blue, blue-violet, purple, and red-violet. This is what I did in *Not Just Huckleberry Pie*.

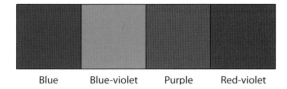

| Blue | Blue-violet | Purple | Red-violet |

These are simple ways to use a color wheel. There are others. But the point is that the color wheel is a tool. It can give you information you don't have to figure out yourself.

Having said that, you can always color outside the lines. Color combinations such as yellow and red (*Strawberry Shortcake and Chocolate Truffles*, page 29) or pink and brown (*Almost Neapolitan*, page 21) are very attractive and popular, but they don't follow any of the above guidelines.

Make quilts that please you. Use colors that you like. When you get bored with those colors, look at the color wheel for inspiration. In the meantime, look at quilts in shops, in shows, and in books. When you like the colors, try to figure out why. Perhaps the quilter used complementary pairs or split complementary or analogous colors. Now you can figure that out and use this information in your very own quilts.

VALUE—KEY POINTS

Value is the degree of lightness or darkness of a color. Value and color are related, but they are not the same thing.

Another word for value is contrast. Your blocks need contrast for the designs to appear.

In general, we divide value into three categories: light, medium, and dark. Usually, when fabrics with different values are next to each other in a block or in a quilt, there is contrast.

To determine value, place the fabrics you want to use in a block side by side or overlapping, and step ten or more feet away. If you can't see the contrast from a distance, change one or more of the fabrics so you can.

Preview fabrics for value on a vertical surface, not a horizontal one, so that your perspective is not skewed and every fabric is the same distance from your eyes.

If you like the colors in a quilt, but you are unhappy with the blocks, the problem is value, not color.

Color gets all the credit in a quilt, but value does all the work.

EASY BLOCKS & COMPLEX LOOK

All the quilts in this book use only two simple blocks that are repeated: Half-Square triangles and Four-Patches. Some quilts have only one or the other. Most of the quilts have both. In some of the quilts, I have played with this idea so that the Half-Square triangles and Four-Patches don't look like traditional blocks. Then when I put them together to make a quilt, it looks much more complex than just these two simple blocks.

HALF-SQUARE TRIANGLES

Each project has the specific instructions needed to make Half-Square triangle blocks. I make them a little oversize and trim them. Why? For accuracy and ease in sewing everything together. Half-Square triangles have a tendency to be a little too big or a little too small or to have concave edges or convex edges. It is difficult, when these things happen, to create an accurate block. And, added to these possibilities, we all take a slightly different seam allowance, even if it is supposedly an accurate ¼ inch. Also, we all press a little differently, and some fabrics have more stretch than others. To compensate for all of the above factors, you will make the Half-Square triangles slightly larger than they need to be and then trim them down to the exact size. Rather than adding only ⅞ inch to the

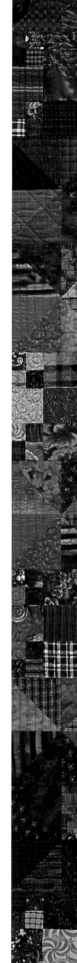

desired finished-size triangle, I add 1 inch to allow the little bit of extra for trimming.

1. Layer 2 squares, right sides together. Mark the diagonal line on the back of the lighter square.

2. Sew the layered squares together. Sew a scant ¼" away from the diagonal line on both sides, and then cut on the diagonal line to make 2 Half-Square triangles. Press the seam allowance, usually toward the darker fabric.

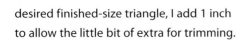

Note

A scant ¼" seam is slightly less than a full, measured ¼" seam, but not so small that it is a ⅛" seam.

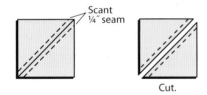

Scant ¼" seam

Cut.

3. To trim the Half-Square triangles, line up the 45° line on a 6" (or larger) bias square ruler or other 6" (or larger) square ruler with the diagonal seam. Trim the top and side just enough to square up the corner.

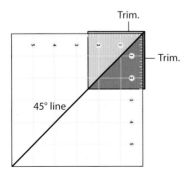

Trim.

Trim.

45° line

4. Remove the ruler, rotate the Half-Square triangle 180°, and again line up the 45° line of the ruler with the diagonal seam. Align the trimmed sides with the desired size on the ruler. Trim the remaining sides.

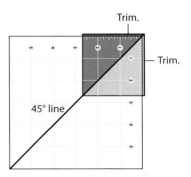

Trim.

Trim.

45° line

SUPPLIES

The following supplies are needed for all the projects:

- **Sewing machine** in good working order.

- **Sewing supplies** you regularly use such as thread, straight pins, scissors, seam ripper, and so forth.

- **Rotary cutting equipment:** mat (18" × 24"), ruler (6" × 24"), and cutter with sharp blade.

- **Bias square ruler,** 6" × 6", or another 6" square ruler. *This is important.*

For several projects, you'll need the following supplies:

- **Square ruler,** 6" × 6" (not the same as a bias square ruler). You may be using this ruler already rather than a bias square ruler. This ruler, with its vertical and horizontal lines as well as its diagonal line, will allow you to cut certain blocks in this quilt to size much easier than a bias square ruler.

- **Bias square ruler,** 8" × 8", or another 8" or larger square ruler. In several quilts, you trim some Half-Square triangles to 6½" × 6½", so a 6" square ruler won't be large enough. A 6" square ruler, however, if you have one, will be easier to handle for trimming the smaller Half-Square triangles.

- **12½" square ruler** This is necessary to cut 10½" squares and to trim large Quarter-Square triangles. *This is important.*

- **6" × 12" ruler** *is useful, but optional*

PROJECTS

The projects in this book are designed so that you can do one of the following:

- Use many fabrics from your stash, giving the quilts a scrappy look.

- Use fewer fabrics and purchase yardage.

- Use a combination of scraps and yardage.

The project instructions include the amount of fabric to buy if you are purchasing, or you can refer to the cutting instructions to see exactly how big each piece of fabric needs to be so you can use fabrics from your stash.

NOTE that the yardage requirements are generous to allow for shrinkage and a cutting mistake or two. If you don't have enough scraps to make a particular quilt, buying fabric will help you build a stash of fabric scraps to make more quilts!

With each quilt, you can practice using color and value effectively. Before you start a project, take a look at the quilts pictured at the end of the project and in the two student challenges to see how some of my students interpreted the project quilts with their own colors:

Triple Berry Tumble *quilt*

riple Berry Tumble combines two complementary colors, red-orange and blue-green. Rich and intensely colorful, this quilt has surprising accents of bright red-orange and blue-green prints.

CUTTING

Red-orange fabrics

■ From each of the 16 red-orange fabrics, cut 1 strip 3½″ × 42″.

From each strip, cut 5 squares 3½″ × 3½″ for a total of 80 squares. You will use 77.

■ From each of the 16 red-orange fabrics, cut 1 strip 2″ × 42″ for Four-Patch blocks.

■ From each of the 16 red-orange fabrics, cut 1 strip 5½″ × 42″.

From each strip, cut 7 squares 5½″ × 5½″ for a total of 112 squares for Half-Square triangle blocks.

■ From the dark red-orange fabrics only, cut an assortment of 72 squares 5″ × 5″.

■ From the medium and/or bright red-orange fabrics only, cut an assortment of 8 squares 5″ × 5″.

Blue-green fabrics

■ From each of the 16 blue-green fabrics, cut 1 strip 3½″ × 42″.

From each strip, cut 5 squares 3½″ × 3½″ for a total of 80 squares for Half-Square triangle blocks. You will use 68.

■ From each of the 16 blue-green fabrics, cut 1 strip 2″ × 42″ for Four-Patch blocks.

■ From each of the 16 blue-green fabrics, cut 1 strip 5½″ × 42″.

From each strip, cut 7 squares 5½″ × 5½″ for a total of 112 squares for Half-Square triangle blocks. You will use 92.

QUILTED BY: Carrie Peterson
FINISHED QUILT SIZE: 90½″ × 90½″

YARDAGE

■ ½ yard of 16 different red-orange fabrics

■ ½ yard of 16 different blue-green fabrics

■ Backing fabric: 8¼ yards (2 horizontal seams)

■ Binding fabric: ¾ yard

■ Batting: 96″ × 96″

Color Code

▢	= Medium and/or Bright Blue-green
▢	= Dark Blue-green
▢	= Medium and/or Bright Red-orange
▢	= Dark Bright Red-orange

hint

Red-orange and blue-green are challenging colors to choose. Be careful not to choose fabrics that are really red or really orange rather than red-orange. Be careful not to choose fabrics that are really blue or really green rather than blue-green. I choose fabrics by looking at both the reds and oranges, then the greens and blues: red fabrics that look orange are probably red-orange; orange fabrics that look red are probably red-orange; blue fabrics that look green are probably blue-green; and green fabrics that look blue are probably blue-green. Try this, and see if it helps you select true red-oranges and blue-greens.

CONSTRUCTION

Make sure your ¼″ seam allowance is accurate —all blocks assume an accurate ¼″ seam.

MAKING HALF-SQUARE TRIANGLE BLOCKS

Using the 5½″ squares, make 92 blue-green Half-Square triangles and 112 red-orange Half-Square triangles.

1. Pair 1 medium and/or bright blue-green 5½″ square and 1 dark blue-green 5½″ square, right sides together. Refer to pages 7–8 for Half-Square triangle construction Steps 1–4.

2. Trim each block to 5″ × 5″.

3. Repeat Steps 1–2, using additional medium and/or bright blue-green squares and dark blue-green squares to make 112 blue-green Half-Square triangles. You need 92.

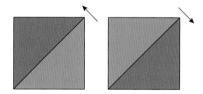

4. Repeat Steps 1–2, using additional medium and/or bright red-orange squares and dark red-orange squares to make 112 red-orange Half-Square triangles.

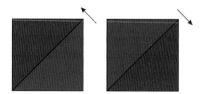

MAKING FOUR-PATCH BLOCKS

Use 16 of the 2″ red-orange strips and 16 of the 2″ blue-green fabrics to make 116 Four-Patch blocks.

1. Pair 1 red-orange fabric strip and 1 blue-green fabric strip, right sides together. Sew the strips together.

Sew strips together.

2. Press seams toward the blue-green fabric. Cut into 15 sections, each 2″ wide. Repeat with the remaining red-orange and blue-green fabric strips.

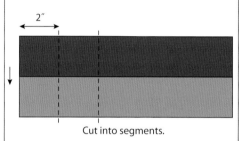

Cut into segments.

3. Arrange 2 segments as shown, and sew together. Make 120 Four-Patch blocks. You need 116 Four-Patch blocks.

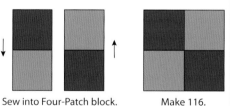

Sew into Four-Patch block.   Make 116.

ASSEMBLING THE BLOCKS

Combine 4 different Four-Patch blocks and 5 different 3½″ squares to make each block. Note the placement of the Four-Patch blocks to create a diagonal pattern of red-orange or blue-green squares.

1. For blocks with a blue-green background, arrange 4 different blue-green 3½″ squares, 1 red-orange 3½″ square, and 4 different Four-Patch blocks.

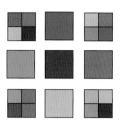

2. Sew together in rows. Press toward the 3½″ squares. Sew rows together, and press. Make 13. Blocks measure 9½″ × 9½″.

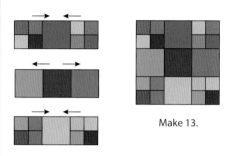

Make 13.

3. For blocks with a red-orange background, arrange 4 different red-orange 3½″ squares, 1 blue-green 3½″ square, and 4 different Four-Patch blocks.

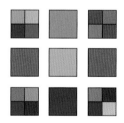

4. Sew together in rows. Press toward the 3½″ squares. Sew rows together, and press. Make 16. Blocks measure 9½″ × 9½″.

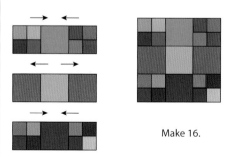

Make 16.

ASSEMBLING THE QUILT TOP

1. Arrange 13 blue-green 9½″ blocks and 92 blue-green Half-Square triangles as shown. Notice the placement of the Half-Square triangles to form a diamond around the 9½″ blocks. Place lower-contrast Half-Square triangles in the positions designated with dots, if possible. Stand back, and look at your arrangement. Balance the eye-catching fabrics.

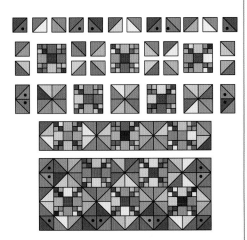

2. Sew the center section (blue-green background) together. Press seams as desired.

3. Arrange 12 dark red-orange 5″ × 5″ squares and 12 red-orange Half-Square triangles for top and bottom rows as shown in the Step 4 diagram. Sew together, and press. Sew to the top and bottom of the center section. Press seams as desired.

4. Arrange 4 medium and/or bright red-orange 5″ × 5″ squares, 12 dark red-orange 5″ × 5″ squares, and 12 red-orange Half-Square triangles for side borders as shown. Sew pieces together, and press. Sew to the sides of the center section. Press seams as desired.

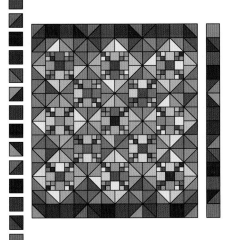

5. Arrange 8 red-orange 9½″ blocks, 40 red-orange Half-Square triangles, and 12 dark red-orange 5″ × 5″ squares for top and bottom rows. Notice the placement of the Half-Square triangles to form a

diamond around the 9½″ blocks. Stand back, look at your arrangement, and balance the eye-catching fabrics. Sew pieces together as shown. Press seams.

6. Arrange 8 red-orange 9½″ blocks, 48 red-orange Half-Square triangles, 36 dark red-orange 5″ × 5″ squares, and 4 medium and/or bright red-orange 5″ × 5″ squares for side borders. Notice the placement of the Half-Square triangles to form a diamond around the 9½″ blocks. Note the placement of the 4 medium and/or bright red-orange squares. Stand back, look at your arrangement, and balance the eye-catching fabrics. Sew pieces together as shown. Press seams.

7. Layer the top with batting and backing. Quilt and bind as desired.

Quilt Assembly Diagram

Triple Berry Tumble at Sunrise

This dessert is quick to prepare, beautiful to look at, incredibly easy to make, and very adaptable. Use whatever berries you have on hand, and if you don't have the ingredients for French Cream—try Cool Whip! Triple Berry Tumble is oh-so-very good to eat, too! Who ever thought a low-calorie dessert could taste this good?

INGREDIENTS

- An assortment of your favorite berries such as strawberries, blueberries, raspberries, or blackberries. Fresh is best, but you can use frozen berries. Taste, and add sugar to sweeten, if desired.

- Angel food cake (purchased or homemade), cut into wedges

- 1 cup heavy whipping cream

- 1 cup sour cream

- Brown sugar

1. To make French Cream combine 1 cup heavy whipping cream (don't whip it) and 1 cup sour cream. Whisk to mix well. Cover and let stand until ready to serve.

2. Place a wedge of angel food cake on a plate. Spoon berries on top. Spoon French Cream over berries. Top with brown sugar sprinkles.

Enjoy!

Fiesta
by Mary Louise Washer.
Quilted by Barbara Dau.
91˝ × 91˝.

Lemon Blueberry Pound Cake *quilt*

emon Blueberry Pound Cake combines two complementary colors, yellow-orange and blue-violet. Very colorful, this quilt has an unusual circular block and circular setting.

QUILTED BY: Carrie Peterson
FINISHED QUILT SIZE: 80½″ × 96½″

YARDAGE

- 13 different blue-violet fabrics, ½ yard each

- 1 different blue-violet fabric, ⅓ yard

- 1 different blue-violet fabric, ¼ yard

- 13 different yellow-orange fabrics, ½ yard each

- 8 different yellow-orange fabrics, ⅓ yard each

- Backing fabric: 8 yards (2 horizontal seams)

- Binding fabric: ¾ yard

- Batting: 86″ × 102″

Color Code

 = Blue-violet

= Yellow-orange

CUTTING

Blue-violet fabrics

- From each of the 13 blue-violet fabrics, cut 1 square 4½″ × 4½″ for a total of 13 squares.

- From each of the 13 blue-violet fabrics, cut 3 strips 2½″ × 42″.

Using these strips, from each of the 13 fabrics, cut 8 squares 2½″ × 2½″ for a total of 104 squares, cut 8 rectangles 2½″ × 4½″ for a total of 104 rectangles, and cut 8 rectangles 2½″ × 6½″ for a total of 104 rectangles.

- From 1 different blue-violet fabric, cut 2 strips 4½″ × 42″.

- From 1 different blue-violet fabric, cut 1 strip 4½″ × 42″.

Draw a diagonal line on the wrong side of the 2½″ × 2½″ squares.

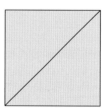

Draw a diagonal line.

Yellow-orange fabrics

- From each of 13 yellow-orange fabrics, cut 4 strips 2½″ × 42″.

Using these strips, from each of the 13 fabrics, cut 44 squares 2½″ × 2½″ for a total of 572 squares, and cut 4 rectangles 2½″ × 4½″ for a total of 52 rectangles.

Draw a diagonal line on the wrong side of 32 squares 2½″ × 2½″ (not all of them, just 32) for each fabric.

Draw a diagonal line.

hint

Blue-violet, sometimes called periwinkle, can be a challenging color to choose. Be careful not to choose fabrics that are too blue or too purple. I start choosing blue-violet by looking at both the blues and the purples (violets) in the fabric store. If there are fabrics in with the blues that look purple or fabrics in with the purples that look blue, they are probably periwinkle.

Likewise, yellow-orange can be a challenging color to choose. If there is a fabric in with the oranges that looks yellow or if there is a fabric in with the yellows that looks orange, these fabrics are probably yellow-orange.

Having said this, try to enjoy the process of choosing your fabrics. This quilt will work even if some fabrics are a little too yellow, too orange, too blue, or too purple. These will add variety and interest to your quilt.

CONSTRUCTION

Make sure your ¼˝ seam allowance is accurate—all blocks assume an accurate ¼˝ seam.

MAKING STAR BLOCKS

Each Star block uses a different blue-violet and yellow-orange fabric combination. From 1 blue-violet fabric, use 1 4½˝ square and 8 matching 2½˝ squares. From 1 yellow-orange fabric, use 4 rectangles 2½˝ × 4½˝ and 4 matching 2½˝ squares for each block.

1. Place 1 blue-violet 2½˝ square to an edge of 1 yellow-orange 2½˝ × 4½˝ rectangle, right sides together. Sew on the diagonal line. Press. Square up the edge of the flipped blue-violet fabric so that it matches the edge of the yellow-orange rectangle, if necessary, and then trim out the back 2 layers of fabric.

 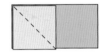 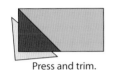

Draw diagonal line.   Stitch on line.   Press and trim.

2. Place another blue-violet 2½˝ square to the opposite edge of the same yellow-orange rectangle, right sides together. Press. Square up the edge, and trim the back 2 layers of fabric. This unit becomes 2 of the Star's points.

Press and trim.

3. Repeat Steps 1 and 2 to sew the remaining 3 rectangles and 6 squares to make additional Star point units.

4. Sew 2 yellow-orange 2½˝ squares to opposite ends of Star point unit. Press toward the squares. Make 2.

5. Sew Star point units to opposite sides of 1 blue-violet 4½˝ square. Press toward the square.

   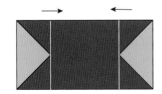

6. Arrange and sew the rows together. Press.

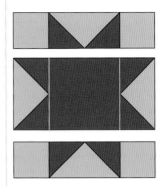 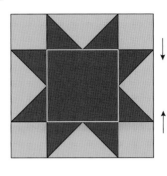

7. Repeat Steps 1–6 to sew additional yellow-orange and blue-violet fabrics to make a total of 13 Star blocks.

MAKING CIRCLE BLOCKS

There are many triangles in this quilt, and they could be made with Half-Square triangle blocks. However, in this quilt, I gave this idea a little twist—although there are triangles, they are made using squares and rectangles.

1. Using 4 blue-violet 2½˝ × 4½˝ rectangles, and 8 yellow-orange 2½˝ squares, make 4 units as shown. Draw diagonal lines on the wrong side of the squares. Sew on drawn lines. Press and square up the edges, and trim back 2 layers of fabric.

 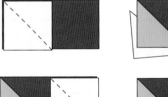

Stitch on line.   Press and trim.

2. Repeat Step 1 using 4 more blue-violet 2½˝ × 4½˝ rectangles and 8 yellow-orange 2½˝ squares to make 4 units as shown.

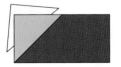 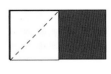
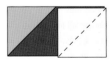 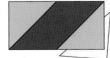

Stitch on line.   Press and trim.

3. Using 4 blue-violet 2½″ × 6½″ rectangles and 8 yellow-orange 2½″ squares, make 4 units as shown.

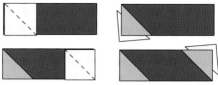

Stitch on line.   Press and trim.

4. Using 4 more blue-violet 2½″ × 6½″ rectangles and 8 yellow-orange 2½″ squares, make 4 units as shown.

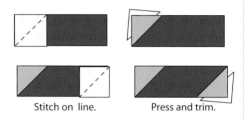

Stitch on line.   Press and trim.

5. Arrange and sew together the Star block, 4½″ units, 6½″ units, and 8 yellow-orange 2½″ squares as shown. Make 1 Circle block.

6. Repeat Steps 1–5 using 96 blue-violet 2½″ × 4½″ rectangles, 96 blue-violet 2½″ × 6½″ rectangles, and 480 yellow-orange 2½″ squares to make a total of 13 Circle blocks. Block measures 16½″ × 16½″.

Make 13.

MAKING FOUR-PATCH BLOCKS

You will make the Four-Patch blocks using leftover yellow-orange and blue-violet 2½″ strips.

As with the Half-Square triangle blocks, I added a little twist in this quilt to the Four-Patches. I placed the leftover yellow-orange strips right-side up (they are longer), and then put the blue-violet strips on top, right sides together. I added blue-violet strips, leaving a small space in between, and continued adding until I sewed the length of the yellow-orange strips. Not all yellow-orange strips were long, but I continued to make pairs of yellow-orange and blue-violet strips until I ran out of either color. I did not cut additional strips.

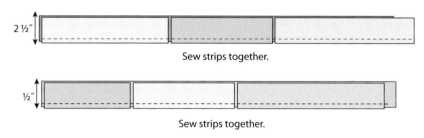

Sew strips together.

Sew strips together.

1. Press all strip sections toward the blue-violet fabrics. Cut into 2½″ sections.

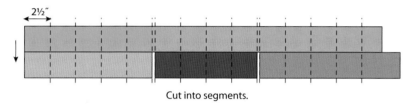

Cut into segments.

2. Arrange 2 segments as shown, and sew together. Press. Make 36 Four-Patch blocks.

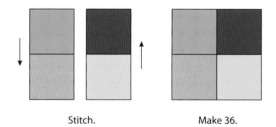

Stitch.   Make 36.

MAKING PLAIN SQUARES

▪ From each of the 13 yellow-orange fabrics that were originally ½ yard, cut 1 strip from the remaining fabric 4½″ × 42″. From each of these strips, cut 9 squares 4½″ × 4½″.

▪ From each of the 8 yellow-orange fabrics, cut 2 strips 4½″ × 42″; using these strips cut 11 squares 4½″ × 4½″. Cut a total of 205 squares. You will use 204.

▪ From 1 of the blue-violet fabrics 4½″ × 42″, cut 8 squares 4½″ × 4½″.

▪ From the other 2 blue-violet fabric strips 4½″ × 42″, cut 16 squares 4½″ × 4½″.

ASSEMBLING THE QUILT TOP

1. Arrange the Circle blocks, Four-Patch blocks, and 4½˝ squares as shown. Quilt will be sewn together in 5 horizontal rows.

2. Sew together 3 Circle blocks, 12 blue-violet squares, and 60 yellow squares to make a horizontal row. Make 2 each of Row 1 (top) and Row 5 (bottom). Press seams as desired.

3. Sew together 2 Circle blocks, 10 Four-Patch blocks, and 38 yellow-orange squares too make Rows 2 and 4. Press.

4. Sew together 3 Circle blocks, 16 Four-Patch blocks, and 16 yellow-orange squares to make Row 3. Press.

5. Sew rows together. Press seams as desired.

6. Layer the top with batting and backing. Quilt and bind as desired.

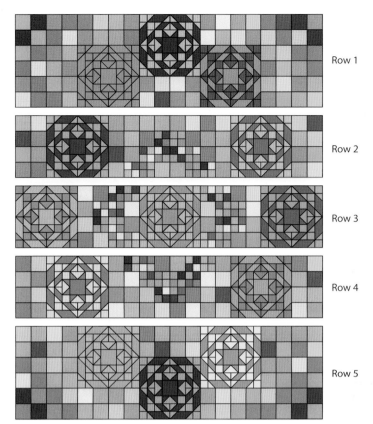

Row 1

Row 2

Row 3

Row 4

Row 5

Quilt Assembly Diagram

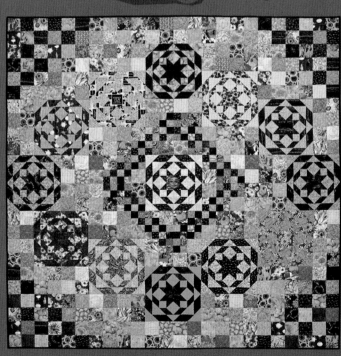

Autumn Treasures by Mary Louise Washer. Quilted by Barbara Dau. 93˝ × 93˝.

Lemon-Blueberry Meringue (or, Where Are the 4 Patches?) by Joan Christ. Quilted by Carrie Peterson. 67˝ × 67˝.

Lemon Blueberry Pound Cake

INGREDIENTS

- ½ cup butter
- 1 cup sugar
- ½ teaspoon vanilla
- 3 eggs
- 1½ cups flour
- ¼ teaspoon baking powder
- ⅛ teaspoon baking soda
- ½ cup lemon yogurt
- 1 teaspoon shredded lemon peel
- 2 tablespoons lemon juice
- ½ cup fresh or frozen blueberries

1. In a bowl, beat butter on medium to high speed for 30 seconds. Gradually add the sugar, beating about 10 minutes or until very light and fluffy. Add the vanilla. Add eggs, 1 at a time, beating 1 minute after each addition and scraping the bowl often.

2. Combine the flour, baking powder, and baking soda. Add this and the yogurt to the egg mixture, alternately, beating on low to medium speed after each addition, just until combined. Add the lemon peel and lemon juice to the batter. Gently fold the blueberries into the batter.

3. Pour into a greased and floured 8″ × 4″ × 2″ or 9″ × 5″ × 3″ loaf pan. Bake at 325° for 60–75 minutes or until a toothpick comes out clean. Cool on a rack 10 minutes. Remove from the pan. Cool before frosting.

CREAM CHEESE FROSTING

- 2 packages cream cheese, 3 ounces each
- ½ cup softened butter
- 2 teaspoons vanilla
- 4½ cups powdered sugar

1. In a bowl, beat together the cream cheese, butter, and vanilla until light and fluffy. Gradually add 2 cups of the powdered sugar, beating well. Gradually beat in enough remaining powdered sugar to make the frosting of spreading consistency.

2. Frost the top of the Lemon Blueberry Pound Cake. You may have extra frosting. Store any leftover cake in the refrigerator.

Almost Neapolitan *quilt*

his quilt features the colors of Neapolitan ice cream—almost. Using browns (dark, chocolate, and medium) and pinks (pastel pinks, dusty pinks, fuchsia pinks, or all of the above), plus a little black added for depth and contrast, you will create a rich, eye-catching, warm-looking quilt.

QUILTED BY: Carrie Peterson
FINISHED QUILT SIZE: 78½" × 78½"

YARDAGE

BLOCK FABRICS

- ⅛ yard each of 5 different pink fabrics
- ½ yard each of 5 different pink fabrics
- ⅓ yard each of 4 different pink fabrics
- ½ yard each of 5 different brown fabrics
- ⅓ yard each of 4 different brown fabrics
- ⅓ yard of 1 black fabric

SASHING AND BORDERS

- ¼ yard of 1 pink fabric (sashing and posts)
- 1¾ yard of 1 black fabric (sashing and inner border)
- Leftover pink block fabrics (middle border)
- ¾ yard of 1 pink fabric (outer border)
- Backing fabric: 5 yards*
   *If fabric is less than 44" you will need 7⅛ yards (2 horizontal seams).
- Binding fabric: ⅔ yard
- Batting: 84" × 84"

Color Code

	= Lightest Pinks (used only in sashing strips)
	= Medium Pinks
	= Dark Pinks
	= Medium, Chocolate, and Dark Browns
	= Black

CUTTING

FOR THE BLOCKS

Pink (⅛ yard) fabric

- From each of 5 pink fabrics, cut 1 strip 3" × 42".

From each strip, cut 2 squares 3" × 3" for a total of 10 squares.

Recut the remainder of each strip to 2½" wide × 22" long approximately.

Draw a diagonal line on the wrong side of the 3" × 3" squares. Draw another set of lines a scant ¼" from the drawn lines—these are your sewing lines. If you have a ¼" presser foot, then you can omit the second set of lines.

Draw a diagonal line.

Pink (½ yard) and Brown (½ yard) fabrics

- From each of 5 pink and 5 brown fabrics, cut 1 strip 6½" × 42".

From each strip, cut 4 rectangles 6½" × 4½" for a total of 20 pink rectangles and 20 brown rectangles.

Open the strips to a single layer. From each, cut 1 rectangle 3" × 6½". Cut each rectangle into 2 squares 3" × 3" for a total of 10 pink squares and 10 brown squares.

Recut the remainder of each strip to 5" wide. Then cut 4 squares 5" × 5" from the strips for a total of 20 pink squares and 20 brown squares.

Draw a diagonal line on the wrong side of the 3" × 3" and 5" × 5" squares.

- From each of 5 pink fabrics and 5 brown fabrics, cut 1 strip 2½" × 42". From each strip, cut 4 rectangles 2½" × 4½" for a total of 20 pink rectangles and 20 brown rectangles.

Cut the remainder of each strip 22" long.

Pink (⅓ yard) and Brown (⅓ yard) fabrics

- From each of 4 pink fabrics and 4 brown fabrics, cut 1 strip 3" × 42".

From each strip, cut 4 squares 3" × 3" for a total of 16 pink squares and 16 brown squares.

Recut the remainder of each strip to 2½" wide.

From these strips, cut 4 squares 2½" × 2½" and 4 rectangles 2½" × 4½" for a total of 16 pink squares, 16 pink rectangles, 16 brown squares, and 16 brown rectangles.

- From each of 4 pink fabrics and 4 brown fabrics, cut 1 strip 5" × 42".

From each strip, cut 4 squares 5" × 5" for a total of 16 pink squares and 16 brown squares.

Draw a diagonal line on the wrong side of the 3" × 3" and 5" × 5" squares.

Black fabric (⅓ yard)

- Cut 1 strip 3" × 42". From that strip, cut 8 squares 3" × 3".

- Cut 2 strips 2½" × 42". Cut these strips on the fold to yield 4 strips approximately 2½" × 21".

FOR THE SASHING AND POSTS

Pink fabric (¼ yard)

■ Cut 2 strips 1¾˝ × 42˝.

From these strips, cut 32 squares 1¾˝ × 1¾˝.

■ Cut 4 squares 3˝ × 3˝.

Draw a diagonal line on the wrong side of each 1¾˝ × 1¾˝ square.

Black fabric

■ Cut 6 strips 3˝ × 42˝.

From these strips, cut 12 rectangles 3˝ × 20½˝.

FOR THE BORDERS

Black fabric (Inner Border)

■ Cut 8 strips 3½˝ × 42˝.

Sew 2 strips end-to-end to make an approximately 84˝ strip. Press. Make 4.

From these strips, cut 2 strips 65½˝ long for the side borders and 2 strips 71½˝ long for the top and bottom borders.

Pink fabric (Middle Border)

■ Choose 8 pink fabrics that were used in the Star blocks.

From each fabric cut 1 strip 2˝ × 42˝. From each strip, cut 4 rectangles 2˝ × 10½˝. Cut a total of 32 strips. Sew pieces randomly end-to-end to make 1 long strip.

From this strip, cut 2 strips 71½˝ long for the side borders and 2 strips 74½˝ long for the top and bottom borders.

Pink fabric (Outer Border)

■ Cut 8 strips 2½˝ × 42˝. Sew 2 strips end-to-end to make an approximately 84˝ strip. Press. Make 4.

From these strips, cut 2 strips 74½˝ long for the side borders and 2 strips 78½˝ long for the top and bottom borders.

CONSTRUCTION

Make sure your ¼˝ seam allowance is accurate—all blocks assume an accurate ¼˝ seam allowance.

MAKING FOUR-PATCH BLOCKS

Use 10 different contrasting pink strips 2½˝ × 22˝ to make 20 Four-Patch blocks.

1. Pair 2 different pink strips, right sides together. Sew strips together.

Sew strips together.

2. Press seams toward the darker fabric. Cut each into 8 sections 2½˝ wide for a total of 20 pairs.

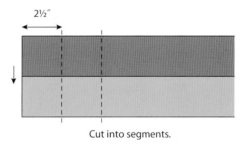

Cut into segments.

3. Arrange 2 segments as shown and sew together. Make 4 identical blocks from each matching pair of strip sets.

Sew into Four-Patch block.   Make 4.

4. Sew the 4 Four-Patch blocks together. Place pink squares so they alternate to make a checkerboard pattern. Repeat steps to make a total of 5 Checkerboard Pink blocks.

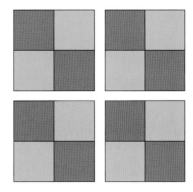 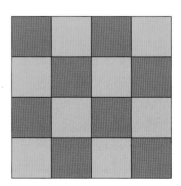

Make 5.

5. Repeat Steps 1–4 using 4 different brown strips 2½″ × 22″ and 4 different black strips 2½″ × 21″ to make 4 Checkerboard Brown blocks.

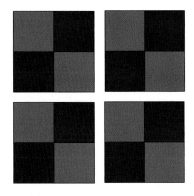

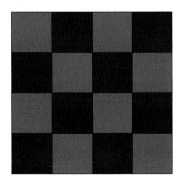

Make 4

MAKING HALF-SQUARE TRIANGLE BLOCKS WITH PINK BACKGROUND

Using 2 pink 3″ squares, 2 different pink 3″ squares, and 4 matching brown 3″ squares, make the small Half-Square triangle blocks. Using 4 matching pink 5″ squares and 4 matching brown 5″ squares, make the large Half-Square triangle blocks.

1. Pair 1 pink 3″ square and 1 brown 3″ square, right sides together. Refer to pages 7–8 for Half-Square triangle construction Steps 1–4.

2. Press the seam allowances toward the darker fabric. Each pair of squares yields 2 Half-Square triangles. Use the remaining 3″ pink and 3″ brown squares to make 8 total small Half-Square triangles.

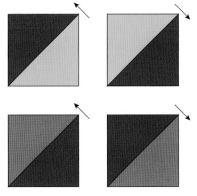

Press. Make a total of 8.

3. Trim each small Half-Square triangle to 2½″ × 2½″.

4. Pair 1 pink 5″ square and 1 brown 5″ square, right sides together. Stitch a scant ¼″ away from the centerline on both sides. Cut on the centerline.

5. Press the seam allowances toward the darker fabric. Each pair of squares yields 2 Half-Square triangles. Use the remaining matching 5″ pink and remaining matching 5″ brown squares to make a total of 8 Half-Square triangles.

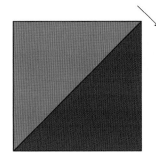

Make 8.

6. Trim each large Half-Square triangle to 4½″ × 4½″.

MAKING HALF-SQUARE TRIANGLE BLOCKS WITH BROWN BACKGROUND

Using 4 matching pink 3″ squares, 2 brown 3″ squares, and 2 black 3″ squares, make the small Half-Square triangle blocks. Using 4 matching pink 5″ squares and 4 matching brown 5″ squares, make the large Half-Square triangle blocks.

1. Pair 1 pink 3″ square and 1 brown 3″ square, right sides together. Refer to pages 7–8 for Half-Square triangle construction Steps 1–4.

2. Press the seam allowances toward the darker fabric. Each pair of squares yields 2 Half-Square triangles. Use 1 of the remaining pink 3″ squares and the remaining brown 3″ square to make 4 small Half-Square triangles.

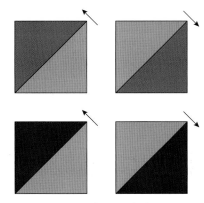

Press. Make a total of 8.

3. Pair 1 pink 3″ square and 1 black 3″ square, right sides together. Stitch a scant ¼″ away from the centerline on both sides. Cut on the centerline.

4. Press seam allowances toward the black fabric. Each pair of squares yields 2 Half-Square triangles. Use the remaining pink 3″ square and the remaining black 3″ square to make a total of 4 small Half-Square triangles.

5. Trim all of the small Half-Square triangles to 2½″ × 2½″.

6. Pair 1 pink 5″ square and 1 brown 5″ square, right sides together. Stitch a scant ¼″ away from the centerline on both sides. Cut on the centerline.

7. Press seams toward the darker fabric. Each pair of squares yields 2 Half-Square triangles. Using the remaining matching 5″ pink squares and the remaining matching 5″ brown squares, make a total of 8 Half-Square triangles.

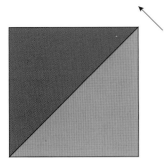

Make 8.

8. Trim these Half-Square triangles to 4½″ × 4½″.

ASSEMBLING THE BLOCKS

PINK BACKGROUND BLOCK

1. Arrange 1 checkerboard pink block, 4 matching pink/brown small Half-Square triangles, 4 different matching pink/ brown small Half-Square triangles, 8 matching pink/brown large Half-Square triangles, 4 matching brown 2½″ × 4½″ rectangles, 4 matching brown 2½″ squares, 4 matching pink 2½″ × 4½″ rect-angles, and 4 matching pink 4½″ × 6½″ rectangles as shown.

2. Sew 4 large Half-Square triangles, 4 brown squares, and 4 small Half-Square triangles, 2 of each variation, together as shown. Press as desired.

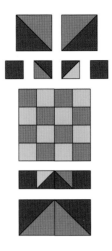

3. Sew 2 large pink rectangles and 2 large Half-Square triangles as shown. Press. Make 2.

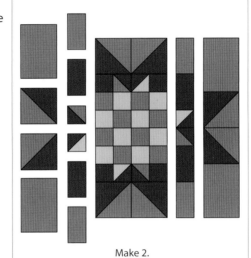

Make 2.

4. Sew 2 pink rectangles, 2 brown rect-angles, and 2 small Half-Square triangles as shown in Step 3. Press. Make 2.

5. Sew sections from Steps 2, 3, and 4 together as shown. Press. Repeat to make 5 pink background blocks. Blocks measure 20½″ × 20½″.

BROWN BACKGROUND BLOCK

1. Arrange 1 checkerboard brown/black block, 4 matching brown/pink small Half-Square triangles, 4 matching black/pink small Half-Square triangles, 8 matching pink/brown large Half-Square triangles, 4 matching pink 2½″ × 4½″ rectangles, 4 matching pink 2½″ squares, 4 matching

brown 2½″ × 4½″ rectangles, and 4 matching pink 4½″ × 6½″ rectangles as shown.

2. Sew 4 large Half-Square triangles, 4 pink squares, and 4 small Half-Square triangles, 2 of each variation, together as shown. Press as desired.

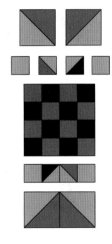

3. Sew 2 large brown rectangles and 2 large Half-Square triangles as shown. Press. Make 2.

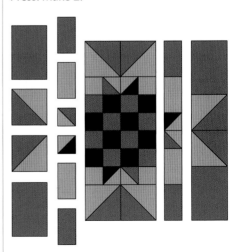

4. Sew 2 brown rectangles, 2 pink rectangles, and 2 small Half-Square triangles as shown in Step 3. Press. Make 2.

5. Sew sections from Steps 2, 3, and 4 together as shown in Step 3. Press. Repeat to make 5 brown background blocks. Blocks measure 20½″ × 20½″.

MAKING SASHING AND POST STARS

Use 12 black 3″ × 20½″ rectangles and 32 pink 1¾″ squares to make the points for the Stars.

1. Place 1 pink 1¾″ square to 1 edge of 1 black 3″ × 20½″ rectangle. Sew on the diagonal line. Press. If necessary, square up the edge of the flipped pink fabric so that it matches the edge of the black rectangle. Then trim out the back 2 layers of fabric.

Stitch on line.

Press and trim.

2. Place another pink 1¾″ square to the opposite edge of the same black rectangle. Sew on the diagonal line. Press. If necessary, square up the edge of the flipped pink fabric so that it matches the edge of the black rectangle. Then trim out the back 2 layers of fabric. This unit becomes 2 of the Star's points. Make 8.

Stitch on line.

Press and trim.

Make 8.

3. Repeat Steps 1 and 2 to sew 4 pink 1¾″ squares to 1 black 3″ × 20½″ rectangle. Press. Make 4.

Make 4.

ASSEMBLING THE QUILT TOP

Arrange the Star blocks, sashing strips, and 3″ pink squares as shown in the Quilt Assembly Diagram. Note the placement of the Star blocks with brown backgrounds, the Star blocks with pink backgrounds, the pink Star points on the ends of the black sashing rectangles, and the black sashing rectangles with pink Star points on both ends.

1. Sew 3 Star blocks and 2 sashing rectangles together in rows. Press seams toward the sashing rectangles. Make 3.

2. Sew the 3 sashing rectangles and 2 pink 3″ squares in rows. Press seams toward the sashing rectangles. Make 2.

3. Sew rows together. Press seams as desired.

ADDING THE BORDERS

1. Fold the quilt top to find midpoints on the sides, and mark with pins. Fold the 65½″ black strips to find midpoints, and mark with pins. With right sides together, match the pins, match and pin the ends of the border strips and the quilt top, and put pins at the approximate quarter points. Sew a 65½″ black strip to each side of the quilt top. In a similar manner, matching midpoints, quarter points, and ends, sew the black 71½″ strips to the top and bottom edges of the quilt top. Press seams toward the borders.

Quilt Assembly Diagram

2. Sew 1 pink 71½" pieced border strip to each side of the quilt top, matching midpoints, quarter points, and ends. Sew the pink 74½" pieced border strips to the top and bottom of the quilt top. Press seams toward the pink pieced borders.

3. Sew 1 pink 74½" outer border strip to each side of the quilt top, matching midpoints, quarter points, and ends. Sew the pink 78½" outer border strips to the top and bottom of the quilt top. Press seams toward the pink pieced borders.

4. Layer the top with batting and backing. Quilt and bind as desired.

Gumdrops by Rachel Barsness. Quilted by Carrie Peterson. 66″ × 86″.

Neapolitan Ice Cream Embellishments

- Purchase a half-gallon of Neapolitan ice cream and embellish as you choose:

- Drizzle hot fudge sauce over your ice cream,

  and/or

- Drizzle caramel sauce over your ice cream,

  and/or

- Spoon strawberry sauce over your ice cream.

- Add whipping cream.

- Sprinkle with colored sprinkles,

  and/or

- chocolate chips or chocolate shavings,

  and/or

- a cherry,

  And of course enjoy!

Chocolate Chip Mint
by Therese Strothman.
76″ × 76″.

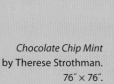

Strawberry Shortcake and Chocolate Truffles *quilt*

his quilt features the colors red, yellow, black, and white. Cheerful and bold, but warm and rich, too, and with a surprising contrast of black and white. I played with colors that don't usually go together

YARDAGE

- 9 different red fabrics, ¼ yard each

- 9 different yellow fabrics, ⅓ yard each

- 1 black fabric (sateen recommended), ⅔ yard

- 1 white fabric (sateen recommended), ⅔ yard

For the border:

- 1 red print fabric, 2⅓ yards

- Backing fabric: 5 yards*

  *If fabric is less than 44″ you will need 7 yards (2 horizontal seams).

- Binding fabric: ⅔ yard

- Batting: 82″ × 82″

Color Code

 = Red

 = Yellow

 = Black

= White

CUTTING

Red and Yellow fabrics

- From 8 of the 9 yellow fabrics, cut 1 strip 2½″ × 42″. (You will not need to cut 1 of the yellow fabrics.)

From each strip, cut 3 rectangles 2½″ × 6½″ for a total of 24 yellow rectangles.

- From each of 9 red and 9 yellow fabrics, cut 1 strip 7″ × 42″.

From each strip, cut 2 squares 7″ × 7″ for a total of 18 red and 18 yellow squares.

Draw a diagonal line on the wrong side of each yellow square.

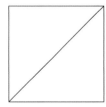

Draw a diagonal line.

From each remaining 7″-wide strip (approximately 28″ length), cut lengthwise 2 strips 3″ × 28″ for a total of 18 red and 18 yellow strips.

From each strip, cut 8 squares 3″ × 3″ for a total of 144 red and 144 yellow squares.

Draw a diagonal line on the wrong side of each yellow square.

Draw a diagonal line.

Black and White fabrics

- From each fabric, cut 8 strips 2½″ × 42″ for a total of 8 black and 8 white strips.

From 1 black strip only, cut 4 squares 2½″ × 2½″.

Draw a diagonal line on the wrong side of each black square.

Borders

Cut the borders lengthwise, parallel to the selvage.

Cut 2 strips 8½″ × 60½″.

Cut 2 strips 8½″ × 76½″.

CONSTRUCTION

Make sure your ¼″ seam allowance is accurate—all blocks assume an accurate ¼″ seam.

MAKING THE BLOCKS

1. Pair 1 red 7″ square and 1 yellow 7″ square, right sides together. Refer to pages 7–8 for Half-Square triangle construction Steps 1–4.

2. Press seams toward the red fabric. Each pair of squares yields 2 Half-Square triangles. Use the remaining red 7″ and yellow 7″ squares to make a total of 36 Half-Square triangles.

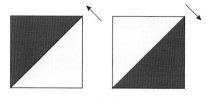

Make 36.

3. Trim each Half-Square triangle to 6½″ × 6½″.

4. Pair 1 red 3″ square and 1 yellow 3″ square, right sides together. Refer to pages 7–8 for Half-Square triangle construction Steps 1–4.

5. Press seams toward the red fabric. Each pair of squares yields 2 Half-Square triangles. Use the remaining red 3″ and yellow 3″ squares to make a total of 288 Half-Square triangles. You will use 276.

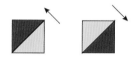

Make 288 (276 needed for quilt).

6. Trim these Half-Square triangles to 2½″ × 2½″.

ASSEMBLING THE BLOCKS

1. Arrange 1 Half-Square triangle 6½″ and 7 Half-Square triangles 2½″ as shown.

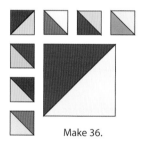

Make 36.

2. Sew units together as shown. Press.

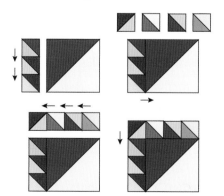

3. Repeat to make 36 blocks total.

FILLER UNITS

1. Pair 1 yellow rectangle 2½″ × 6½″ with 1 Half-Square triangle 2½″ × 2½″. Sew together. Repeat with 11 more yellow rectangles and 2½″ Half-Square triangles. Make 12 total. This is Filler A.

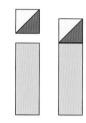

2. Pair 1 yellow rectangle 2½″ × 6½″ with 1 Half-Square triangle 2½″ × 2½″. Sew together. Note that this unit looks different than the Step 1 unit. Repeat with the 11 remaining yellow rectangles and 2½″ Half-Square triangles. Make 12 total. This is Filler B.

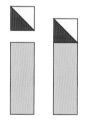

CHECKERBOARD WITH HALF-FOUR-PATCH UNITS

1. Sew 1 black and 1 white strip, right sides together. Press seams toward the black fabric. Cut each strip set into 16 Half-Four-Patch units 2½″ wide.

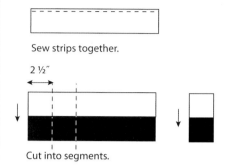

Sew strips together.

2 ½″

Cut into segments.

2. Repeat with the remaining 7 black and 7 white strips. Cut a total of 128 units. You will use 114. You will have a few extra units, even though 1 black strip is shorter than the rest.

ASSEMBLING THE QUILT TOP

Arrange 4 blocks.

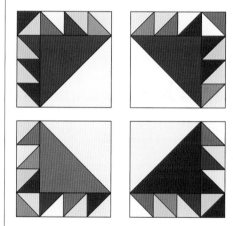

note:

You will have extra 2½″ Half-Square triangles that will be used for the Filler units.

1. Sew and flip a black square. Place 1 black 2½″ square on the block, right sides together. Stitch on the diagonal line. Make 4.

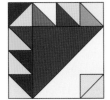 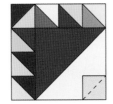

Draw a diagonal line.   Stitch on line.

2. Press the seams in opposite directions (2 toward the black triangle, 2 toward the yellow fabric) so that they will oppose (nest) when you sew these 4 blocks together. If necessary, square up the edge of the flipped black fabric so that it matches the block edge. Then trim out the back 2 layers of fabric.

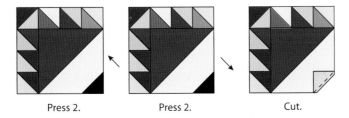

Press 2.   Press 2.   Cut.

3. Sew together 4 blocks with black Half-Square triangles to make the Center Block unit. Press.

4. Sew 4 Half-Four-Patch units together end-to-end. Press seams toward the black squares. Make 2. Sew to side of Center block. Press toward black-and-white squares.

5. Sew 5 Half-Four-Patch units together end-to-end. Press seams toward the black squares. Make 2. Sew to top and bottom of Center block. Press.

6. Refer to Step 7 diagram to arrange 2 blocks, 1 Filler A unit, and 1 Filler B unit. Sew together, pressing seams toward the filler units. Press the center seam as desired. Make 2.

7. Sew these units to opposite sides of the Center block unit. Press seams toward the black-and-white squares.

8. Arrange 4 blocks, 1 Filler A unit, and 1 Filler B unit. Sew together, pressing seams toward the filler units. Press the center seam as desired. Make 2.

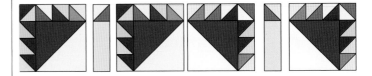

9. Sew these units to the top and bottom of the Center block unit. Press seams toward the black-and-white squares and fillers.

10. Sew 9 Half-Four-Patch units together end-to-end. Press seams toward the black squares. Make 2. Sew these units to the sides of the Center block unit. Press.

11. Sew 10 Half-Four-Patch units together end-to-end. Press seams toward the black squares. Make 2. Sew these units to the top and bottom of the Center block unit. Press.

12. Arrange 4 blocks, 2 Filler A units, and 2 Filler B units. Sew together, pressing seams toward the filler units. Press the center seam as desired. Make 2.

13. Sew these units to opposite sides of the Center block unit. Press seams toward the black-and-white squares.

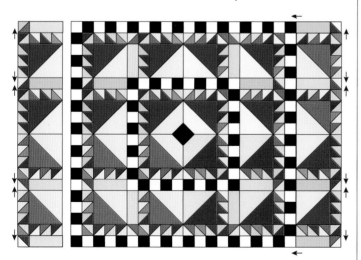

14. Arrange 6 blocks, 2 Filler A units, and 2 Filler B units. Sew together, pressing seams toward the filler units. Press the center seam as desired. Make 2.

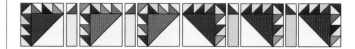

15. Sew these units to the top and bottom of the Center block unit. Press seams toward the black-and-white squares and fillers.

16. Sew 14 Half-Four-Patch units together end-to-end. Press seams toward the black squares.

17. Sew the 14 Half-Four-Patch unit sections to the sides of the Center block unit as shown in the Quilt Assembly Diagram.

18. Sew 15 Half-Four-Patch units together end-to-end. Press seams toward the black squares.

19. Sew the 15 Half-Four-Patch unit sections to the top and bottom of the Center block unit as shown in the Quilt Assembly Diagram. Press seams toward the black-and-white squares.

ADDING THE BORDERS

1. Fold the quilt top to find midpoints on the sides, and mark with pins. Fold the red 60½″ border strips to find midpoints, and mark with pins. With right sides together, match the pins, match and pin the ends of the border strips and the quilt top, and put pins at the approximate quarter points. Sew 1 red 60½″ border strip to each side of the quilt top. Press seams toward the border strips.

2. In a similar manner, matching midpoints, quarter points, and ends, sew the 76½″ red border strips to the top and bottom edges of the quilt top. Press seams toward the borders. See the Quilt Assembly Diagram, right.

3. Layer the top with batting and backing. Quilt and bind as desired.

Quilt Assembly Diagram

Strawberry Shortcake in the Carolinas by Ann Elizabeth Rindge. 51″ × 51″.

The *Antioxidant Quilt* by Peggy Roebuck Jarrett. Quilted by Sue Lohse. 70″ × 70″.

City Life by Mary Louise Washer. Quilted by Barbara Dau. 75″ × 75″.

14-Carat Carrot Cake by Cate Franklin. Quilted by Carrie Peterson. 74″ × 74″.

Strawberry Shortcake

INGREDIENTS

- 2 cups flour
- 2 tablespoons sugar
- 3 teaspoons baking powder
- 1 teaspoon salt
- ⅓ cup shortening (Crisco)
- 1 cup milk
- 1 quart or more of strawberries
- Butter
- Whipped cream

If strawberries are not sweet, slice them, sprinkle them with sugar, and let them stand 1 hour. This is a trick my mother taught me. Your strawberries will become sweet and juicy!

1. Measure flour, sugar, baking powder, and salt into a bowl. Cut in the shortening until the mixture looks well blended. Stir in milk just until blended.

2. Using a large spoon, place 6 heaping spoonfuls of dough onto a greased cookie sheet. Each spoonful of dough will make a shortcake. Bake 15–20 minutes at 450°. The shortcakes should be golden brown. Check a shortcake to be sure it's done by piercing the center with a toothpick. If the toothpick comes out clean, the shortcake is done. Remove shortcakes from the cookie sheet immediately.

3. Split the shortcakes while warm. Spread with butter. Fill with berries, and put more berries on top. Add whipped cream.

WHIPPED CREAM

- 1 pint heavy whipping cream
- 2 tablespoons powdered sugar or regular sugar
- 2 teaspoons real vanilla extract

Whip cream until soft peaks form. Add the sugar and vanilla. Continue whipping until stiff peaks form.

Makes 8 servings.

Using your favorite recipe, make chocolate truffles to go with your strawberry shortcake, or purchase truffles at your favorite candy store.

Enjoy!

Banana Split *quilt*

 his quilt features six complementary colors and two values. The complements are red and green, yellow and purple, and orange and blue. The warm colors—red, yellow, and orange—are featured in light values only. I chose pink (light red), peach (light orange), and light yellow fabrics. The cool colors—green, blue, and purple—are featured in medium values only. I also included many medium- to large-scale prints, plaids, and stripes in my fabric choices, not just small- and medium-scale fabrics.

QUILTED BY: Carrie Peterson
FINISHED QUILT SIZE: 83" × 83"

YARDAGE

Remember to choose many medium- to large-scale print, plaid, and striped fabrics.

- ⅓ yard of 18 different light fabrics, 6 pink, 6 peach, and 6 light yellow

- ½ yard each of 18 different medium fabrics, 6 medium green, 6 medium purple, 6 medium blue. The border will be created using green, purple, and blue fabrics.

- Backing fabric: 7½ yards (2 horizontal seams)

- Binding fabric: ¾ yard

- Batting : 89" × 89"

Color Code

▨	= Pink
▨	= Peach
☐	= Light Yellow
▨	= Medium Green
■	= Medium Purple
▨	= Medium Blue

CUTTING

Light fabrics

- From each of the 18 light fabrics, cut 1 strip 4½" × 42".

From each 4½"-wide strip, cut 5 squares 4½" × 4½" for a total of 90 squares, and 3 squares 4" × 4" for a total of 54 squares. Set the 4" squares aside.

Draw a diagonal line on the wrong side of each light 4½" square.

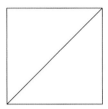

Draw a diagonal line.

- From each of the 18 light fabrics, cut 1 strip 3½" × 42".

From each 3½"-wide strip, cut 6 squares 3" × 3" for a total of 108 squares. Cut these squares once diagonally to make 216 triangles. Set these aside.

Cut each of the remaining 3½"-wide strips in half lengthwise to make 2 strips of each 1¾" × approximately 24" long. These will be used in Four-Patch blocks.

Medium fabrics

- From each of the 18 medium fabrics, cut 1 strip 4½" × 42".

From each 4½"-wide strip, cut 5 squares 4½" × 4½" for a total of 90 squares and 3 squares 4" × 4" for a total of 54 squares. Set the 4" squares aside.

Draw a diagonal line on the wrong side of each light 4½" square.

- From each of the 18 medium fabrics, cut 1 strip 3½" × 42".

From each 3½"-wide strip, cut 6 squares 3" × 3" for a total of 108 squares. Cut these squares once diagonally to make 216 triangles. Set these aside.

Cut each of the remaining 3½"-wide strips in half lengthwise to make 2 strips of each 1¾" × approximately 24" long. These will be used in Four-Patch blocks.

Borders

- From 8 of the darker medium fabrics (blues, purples, greens), cut 1 strip 8½" × 42".

Cut each strip into 2 big rectangles 8½" × 21". Piece 15 of these rectangles together end-to-end to create 1 very long strip.

From this strip, cut 1 border 8½" × 67". Label this border #1, and label "Top" where you began.

Cut another border 8½" × 83". Label this border #2, and label "Top" where you began.

Cut another border 8½" × 67". Label this border #3, and label "Top" where you began.

Cut the final border 8½" × 83". Label this border #4, and label "Top" where you began.

CONSTRUCTION

Make sure your ¼˝ seam allowance is accurate—all blocks assume an accurate ¼˝ seam.

MAKING HALF-SQUARE TRIANGLES

1. Pair 1 pink 4½˝ square with 1 green 4½˝ square, right sides together. Refer to pages 7–8 for Half-Square triangle construction Steps 1–4.

2. Press the seam toward the medium fabric. Each pair of squares yields 2 Half-Square triangles. Pair additional 4½˝ pink and green squares, 4½˝ peach and blue squares, and 4½˝ yellow and purple squares. Notice that you are pairing complementary colors only. You will make 60 pink/green Half-Square triangles, 60 peach/blue Half-Square triangles, and 60 yellow/purple Half-Square triangles.

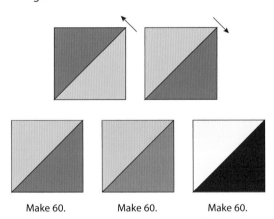

| Make 60. | Make 60. | Make 60. |

3. Trim each Half-Square triangle to 4˝ × 4˝.

MAKING FOUR-PATCHES

1. Pair 1 pink and 1 green strip, right sides together. Sew strips together.

Sew strips together.

2. Press toward the green strip. Cut this into 12 sections, 1¾˝ wide. You may need to use part of the matching pink and matching green strips, or you may not.

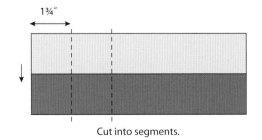

1¾˝

Cut into segments.

3. Pair additional pink and green strips, peach and blue strips, and yellow and purple strips. Notice that you are pairing complementary colors only. Press toward the medium fabrics. Cut each strip set into 12 sections 1¾˝ wide. Use part of the second same strips, if needed. Cut a total of 216 Four-Patch sections 1¾˝ wide.

4. Arrange and sew 2 segments together. Press. Make 100 Four-Patch blocks.

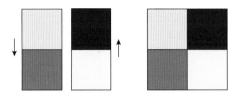

Sew into Four-Patch block. Make 100.

MAKING FOUR-PATCH-IN-A-SQUARE BLOCKS

1. Choose 1 Four-Patch block, 2 light triangles, and 2 medium triangles. Sew the medium triangles to opposite sides of the Four-Patch block. If possible, sew different colors next to each other. Press seams toward the triangle. Trim the points in line with the edge of the Four-Patch block.

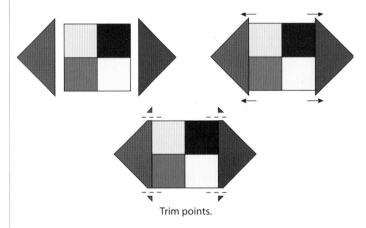

Trim points.

2. Sew the light triangles to opposite sides of the Four-Patch block. If possible, sew different colors next to each other. Press seams toward the triangle. Make 100.

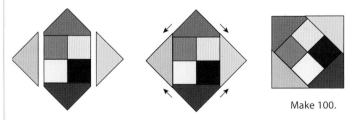

Make 100.

3. Trim the Four-Patch-in-a-Square block to 4˝ × 4˝.

MAKING SNAIL'S TRAIL BLOCKS

1. Arrange 4 Four-Patch-in-a-Square blocks, 4 Half-Square triangles, and 1 square 4″ × 4″. Make a Snail's Trail block. Note the placement of the light and medium fabrics.

2. Sew units together in rows, pressing seams toward the Half-Square triangles.

3. Sew rows together to create the Snail's Trail block. Press seams toward the Half-Square triangle middle row. Repeat to make 25 Snail's Trail blocks.

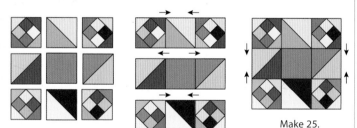

Make 25.

MAKING SASHING SECTIONS

Choose 2 Half-Square triangles and 1 square 4″ × 4″. Sew together. Note the placement of light and medium fabrics. Press seams toward the 4″ square. Make 40 sashing sections.

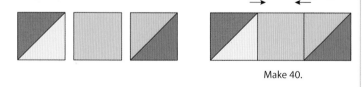

Make 40.

ASSEMBLING THE QUILT TOP

1. Refer to the Quilt Assembly Diagram, right. Arrange the 25 Snail's Trail blocks, 40 sashing sections, and 16 squares 4″ × 4″.

2. Sew together in horizontal rows. Press seams toward the sashing sections.

3. Sew the rows together. Press seams toward the sashing sections.

ADDING THE BORDERS

1. Refer to the Quilt Assembly Diagram. Fold the quilt top to find midpoints on the sides, and mark with pins. Fold the 66½″ border strips to find midpoints, and mark with pins. With right sides together, match the pins, match and pin the ends of the border strips and the quilt top, and put pins at the approximate quarter points. Note the sewing order in the following steps.

2. Sew the #1 border strip to the left side of the quilt top with the "Top" edge at the upper left side of the quilt top.

3. Sew the #3 border strip to the right side of the quilt top, with the "Top" edge at the bottom right side of the quilt top. Press seams toward the borders.

4. In a similar manner, matching midpoints, quarter points, and ends, sew the 82½″ border strips to the top and bottom edges of the quilt top, noting the sewing order in the following steps.

5. Sew the #2 border strip to the bottom of the quilt top with the "Top" edge at the lower left side of the quilt top (with side borders now added).

6. Sew the #4 border strip to the top of the quilt top with the "Top" edge at the upper right side of the quilt top (with side borders now added). Press seams toward the borders.

7. Layer the top with batting and backing. Quilt and bind as desired.

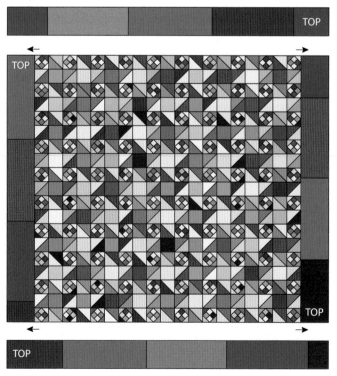

Quilt Assembly Diagram

Strawberry Banana Split by Suzanne Barsness. Quilted by Carrie Peterson. 79˝ × 79˝.

Banana Split

INGREDIENTS

- One ripe banana

- Chocolate, coffee or strawberry, and vanilla ice cream

- Marshmallow, chocolate or hot fudge, and caramel toppings

- Whipped cream

- Nuts, maraschino cherries, and colorful sprinkles to embellish

1. Slice the banana horizontally in half. Place in a bowl or on a plate.

2. Place a scoop of chocolate, then coffee or strawberry, then vanilla ice cream on the banana. Pour marshmallow sauce over the chocolate ice cream, chocolate or hot fudge sauce over the coffee or strawberry ice cream, and caramel sauce over the vanilla ice cream.

3. Add whipped cream, then nuts, cherries, and sprinkles if desired.

Enjoy!

Snips and Snails and Puppy Dog Tails
by Dorothy Finley.
Quilted by Sue Lohse.
67″ × 67″.

Pistachio Almond Cake *quilt*

his quilt was inspired by three things—my students, who asked me why I never made a green quilt; the elegant green floors and accessories in a model home that made me realize green could look really good; and a bouquet of flowers featuring fuchsia, periwinkle, orange, and gold blossoms against a beautiful background of green leaves. Pistachio Almond Cake was inspired by my web designer, Kim Jackson, and one of my students, Joan Christ. After Kim suggested Pistachio Cake, Joan told me that her daughter Susanne had just made one! So thanks to a wonderful team, it's now time to sew your very own *Pistachio Almond Cake Quilt* and to eat Pistachio Almond Cake, too. Enjoy!

QUILTED BY: Carrie Peterson
FINISHED QUILT SIZE: 80½" × 80½"

YARDAGE

Do you want your quilt to be scrappy like mine, or not? You will have a choice.

For a scrap quilt, you will need

- ¼ yard each of 8 different medium fuchsia (bright pink) fabrics
- ¼ yard each of 8 different medium gold fabrics
- ¼ yard each of 8 different medium bright orange fabrics
- ⅛ yard each of 8 different medium bright blue-violet (periwinkle) fabrics
- ¼ yard each of 32 different green fabrics in dark green, sage green, and medium green, but not bright green, not light green, and not Starbucks apron (Kelly) green

For a quilt that has just a few fabrics, you will need

- 1 yard of 1 medium fuchsia fabric
- ½ yard of 1 medium gold fabric
- ½ yard of 1 medium bright orange fabric
- ⅞ yard of 1 medium bright blue violet (periwinkle) fabric
- ¼ yard each of 32 different green fabrics in dark green, sage green, and medium green, but not bright green, not light green, and not Starbucks apron (Kelly) green

It is very pleasing even if you use only a single fabric for the other colors to use a variety of green fabrics for interest rather than just a single green fabric.

- Border fabric: 1⅞ yards
- Corner blocks: Made with leftover green fabrics
- Backing fabric: 5 yards*
  *If fabric is less than 44" you will need 7¼ yards (2 horizontal seams).
- Binding fabric: ¾ yard
- Batting: 86" × 86"

Color Code

■	= Fuchsia
□	= Gold
■	= Blue Violet
■	= Orange
■	= Greens

CUTTING

Fuchsia fabrics

■ Scrap Quilt (assorted fabrics)

From each of 8 fabrics, cut 4 squares 5½" × 5½".

From assorted fuchsia fabric, cut a total of 4 squares 4½" × 4½" and a total of 2 squares 3" × 3".

■ Single Fuchsia fabric

Cut 5 strips 5½" × 42". From this strip, cut 32 squares 5½" × 5½".

Cut 1 strip 4½" × 42". From this strip, cut 4 squares 4½" × 4½" and 2 squares 3" × 3".

Draw a diagonal line on the wrong side of each 5½" and 3" square. Do not mark the back of the 4½" squares.

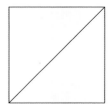

Draw a diagonal line.

Gold fabrics

■ Scrap Quilt (assorted fabrics)

From each of 8 fabrics, cut 1 or 2 squares 5½" × 5½" for a total of 10 squares.

From each of 4 fabrics, cut 1 square 4½" × 4½".

■ Single Gold fabric

Cut 2 strips 5½" × 42". From this strip, cut 10 squares 5½" × 5½".

Cut 1 strip 4½" × 42". From this strip, cut 4 squares 4½" × 4½".

Draw a diagonal line on the wrong side of each 5½" square only.

Orange fabrics

■ Scrap Quilt (assorted fabrics)

From each of 8 orange fabrics, cut 1 or 2 squares 5½" × 5½" for a total of 12 squares.

- Single Orange fabric

Cut 2 strips 5½" × 42". From this strip, cut 12 squares 5½" × 5½".

Draw a diagonal line on the wrong side of each 5½" square.

Blue-Violet fabrics

- Scrap Quilt (assorted fabrics)

From each of 8 fabrics, cut 1 strip 2½" × 42" for a total of 8 strips to make Four-Patch blocks.

- Single Blue-Violet fabric

Cut 8 strips 2½" × 42" for the Four-Patch blocks and Half-Four-Patch blocks.

Green fabrics

In this quilt 32 fabrics are used. Use assorted greens to cut the following:

- Cut a total of 13 strips 4½" × 42". From these strips, cut 89 squares 4½" × 4½". Of these squares, 16 will be used in the border corner blocks, and the remainder will be used in the quilt top. Cut a total of 16 rectangles 2½" × 4½".

- Cut a total of 10 strips 2½" × 42". From 2 of these strips, cut 24 squares 2½" × 2½". The remaining 8 strips will be combined with the blue-violet 2½" strips to make Four-Patch blocks and Half-Four-Patch blocks.

- Cut a total of 10 strips 5½" × 42". From these strips, cut 54 squares 5½" × 5½". Of these squares, 10 will become the gold Quarter-Square triangle blocks, 8 will become the fuchsia Half-Square triangle blocks, 24 will become the fuchsia Quarter-Square triangle blocks, and 12 will become the orange Half-Square triangle blocks.

- Cut 2 squares 3" × 3" from the above fabric leftovers.

CONSTRUCTION

Make sure your ¼" seam allowance is accurate—all blocks assume an accurate ¼" seam.

MAKING HALF-SQUARE TRIANGLES

1. Pair 1 gold 5½" square with 1 green 5½" square, right sides together. Refer to pages 7–8 for Half-Square triangle construction Steps 1–4.

2. Press the seam toward the green fabric. Each pair of squares yields 2 Half-Square triangles. Pair 9 additional gold 5½" squares with 9 green 5½" squares. Press.

3. Pair 32 fuchsia 5½" squares with 32 green 5½" squares. Pair 12 orange 5½" squares with 12 green 5½" squares to make additional Half-Square triangles. You will make 64 fuchsia/green Half-Square triangles and 24 orange/green Half-Square triangles. Set aside the 20 gold/green Half-Square triangles and 48 of the fuchsia/green Half-Square triangles.

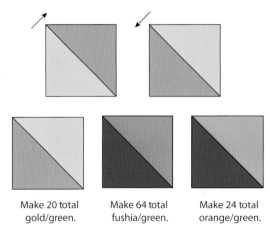

Make 20 total gold/green. Make 64 total fushia/green. Make 24 total orange/green.

4. Trim the 16 fuchsia/green Half-Square triangles and all 24 of the orange/green Half-Square triangles to 4½" × 4½".

5. Repeat Steps 1 and 2 to combine 2 fuchsia 3" squares and 2 green 3" squares to make 4 Half-Square triangles. Trim these to 2½" × 2½".

MAKING QUARTER-SQUARE TRIANGLES

1. Pair 2 gold/green Half-Square triangles, right sides together. Fold back to confirm that golds will be opposite each other and the greens will be opposite each other in the finished block.

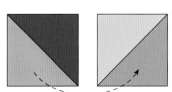

Pair.

2. Draw a diagonal line on the wrong side of 1 of the Half-Square triangles. Stitch a scant ¼" away from the centerline on both sides. Cut on the centerline. Press the seam as desired. Each pair of Half-Square triangles yields 2 Quarter-Square triangles.

Draw a diagonal line.   Sew scant ¼" from center line and cut.

3. Trim these Quarter-Square triangles to 4½" × 4½". Line up the 45° line on a 6" or larger ruler with the diagonal seam. Divide desired block measurement in half. For example trimming the block to 4½" × 4½" half of this is 2¼". Find this measurement on the ruler and lay that point over the center of the block (where seams intersect). Trim the top and side.

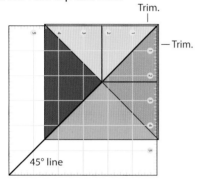

45° line

4. Remove the ruler, rotate the Quarter-Square triangle 180° and line up the 45° line of the ruler with the diagonal seam. Align the trimmed sides with the 4½" marks on the ruler. Trim the remaining sides.

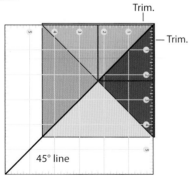

45° line

5. Make 20 gold/green Quarter-Square triangles and 48 fuchsia/green Quarter-Square triangles.

Make 20.   Make 48.

MAKING FOUR-PATCHES AND HALF-FOUR-PATCHES

1. Pair 1 blue-violet and 1 green strip, right sides together. Sew strips together. Make a total of 8 pairs of these strip units.

Sew strips together.

2. Press toward the green strips. Cut each unit into 13 sections 2½" wide, for a total of 104 pairs. Set aside 8 of these units. They will become Half-Four-Patch blocks.

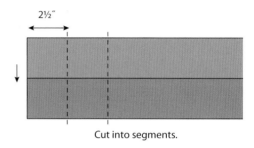

2½"

Cut into segments.

3. Arrange 2 segments as shown, and sew together. Press. Repeat to make a total of 48 Four-Patch blocks.

 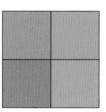

Sew into Four-Patch block.   Make 48.

ASSEMBLING THE QUILT TOP

1. Arrange and sew together 3 green 2½" squares and 1 fuchsia/green Half-Square triangle 2½" × 2½" as shown. Press seams as desired. Make 4.

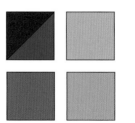 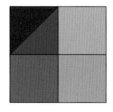

Make 4.

2. Arrange the 4 blocks from Step 1, 1 green 4½" square, and 4 gold/green Quarter-Square triangles. Sew together in horizontal rows. Press seams away from the Quarter-Square triangles in each row. Sew the rows together. Press seams as desired. This section will become the center of your quilt.

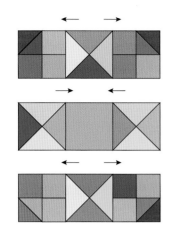

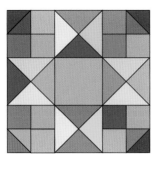

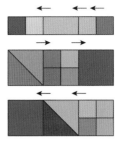

6. Sew the sections on the left and right together in horizontal rows. Press seams in opposite directions from row to row. Sew the rows together. Press seams as desired.

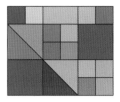

3. Arrange 2 green 2½″ squares, 4 green 2½″ × 4½″ rectangles, 2 Half-Four-Patch units, and 4 fuchsia/green Half-Square triangles. Sew together in horizontal rows. Press seams in opposite directions from row to row. Sew the rows together. Press seams as desired. Make 2.

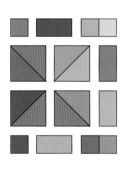
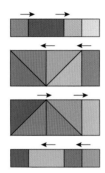

Make 2.

7. Sew the section that includes the 4 fuchsia/green Half-Square triangles and 2 of the green 2½″ × 4½″ rectangles in horizontal rows. Press seams in opposite directions from row to row. Sew the rows together. Press seams.

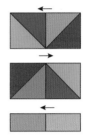

8. Sew the 3 sections together to create a larger section. Press.

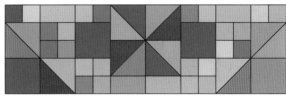

Make 2.

4. Sew units from Step 3 to the sides of the Center section from Step 2 as shown. Press.

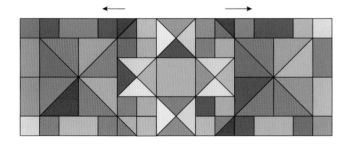

9. Repeat Steps 5–8 to make 2 of these larger sections. Sew them to the top and bottom of the quilt center section. Press seams as desired. This completes the Center section.

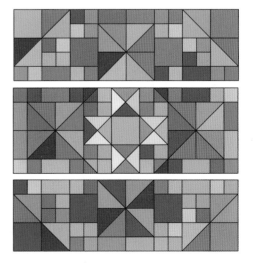

5. Arrange 2 Half-Four-Patch units, 4 green 2½″ × 4½″ rectangles, 4 green 2½″ squares, 4 orange/green Half-Square triangles, 4 fuchsia/green Half-Square triangles, 4 green 4½″ squares, and 4 Four-Patch blocks.

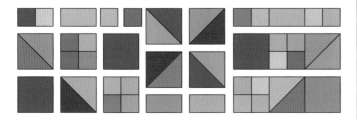

10. Arrange the remaining units around Center block as shown: 40 Four-Patch blocks, 16 orange/green Half-Square triangles, 16 gold/green Quarter-Square triangles, 4 gold 4½″ squares, 48 fuchsia/green Quarter-Square triangles, 4 fuchsia 4½″ squares, and 64 green 4½″ squares.

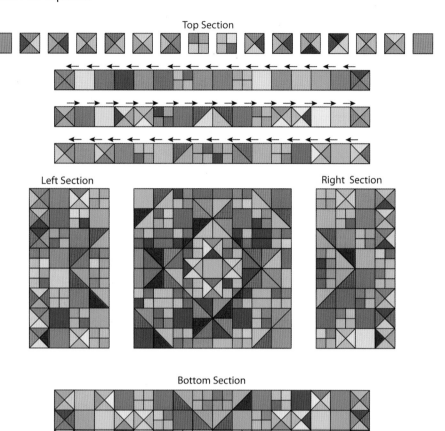

Top Section

Left Section

Right Section

Bottom Section

ADDING THE BORDERS

When sewing borders to a quilt top, mark the quilt and each border piece as follows: Fold the quilt and border pieces to find the midpoints, and mark with pins. Then find the quarter points, and mark with pins. With right sides together, match midpoints, quarter points, and ends prior to sewing the pieces together.

1. From the border fabric, cut 4 large rectangles horizontally (parallel to the selvage) 8½″ × 64½″. These will become your top, bottom, and side borders.

2. Use 4 green 4½″ squares to make 1 large Four-Patch block. Make 4. These will be corner blocks in the borders.

3. With right sides together, sew the border strips to the sides of the quilt top. Press seams toward the borders.

4. Sew a Four-Patch block to opposite ends of the remaining 2 border strips. Press seams toward the border strips. Sew the top and bottom borders to the quilt top. Press.

5. Layer the top with batting and backing. Quilt and bind as desired.

11. Sew the blocks together in horizontal rows. Press seams in opposite directions from row to row.

12. Sew the top 4 rows together to make the Top Section. Press as desired. Repeat to make the Bottom Section. Press.

13. Sew the 8 Left Section rows together. Press seams as desired. Sew the 8 Right Section rows together. Press.

14. Sew the Left Section and Right Section to the Center Section. Press seams as desired. Sew the Top and Bottom Sections to the Center row. Press.

Quilt Assembly Diagram

Pavlova Cake and Mixed Berries
by Cate Franklin.
Quilted by Helene Kempf.
63″ × 63″.

Pistachio Almond Cake Light by Ann Elizabeth Rindge. Quilted by Sue Nebeker. 80˝ × 80˝.

Pistachio Almond Cake

This recipe was inspired by Susanne Everille, Joan's daughter. Thank you, Susanne! This is a delicious, dense cake. It is a little "fussy" to make, but it is so good that it is well worth the effort. I made it in one layer, left it in the pan I cooked it in, and frosted the top. You could remove this cake from the pan when it is cool and then frost the sides, too. Also, this recipe can be cut in half to make a smaller cake. If you do this, use a 9″ × 9″ square pan.

INGREDIENTS

- 2¼ cups of butter (4 sticks and half of a 5th stick), softened
- 2¼ cups sugar
- 6 large eggs
- 1⅓ cups whole pistachios, shelled and unsalted
- 1⅓ cups whole almonds
- 2 oranges
- 2½ teaspoons water
- 1 cup plus 2 tablespoons flour

1. Preheat oven to 325°. Grease and flour a 9″ × 13″ pan.

2. Chop the pistachios and almonds into small pieces, using a food processor or a knife, and set aside. Grate the zest of the oranges to equal approximately 2 tablespoons. Squeeze the oranges to yield approximately ½–¾ cup of juice.

3. Cream the butter and sugar until light and fluffy. Add eggs, 1 at a time, beating after each addition. Add the pistachios and almonds, and stir to blend. Stir in the zest, orange juice, and water. Fold in the flour with a large spoon.

4. Pour into the pan and bake 50–60 minutes, lightly covering the top with foil for the last 10 minutes. You may have to adjust the cooking time, depending on your oven.

5. When you think the cake is done, test with a toothpick or metal knife inserted in the center. It should come out clean, except for maybe a nut, but not with dough on it. If the cake isn't done, continue baking in 5-minute increments until your toothpick or knife comes out clean. Don't overbake because this cake cools in the pan. The cake will be golden brown on top when it is done. Let the cake cool in the pan on a rack or on the top of the stove.

6. Frost the cake with cream cheese frosting. Decorate with leftover pistachio and/or almond pieces, if desired.

CREAM CHEESE FROSTING

- 12 ounces cream cheese (regular, not light), softened
- ¼ cup milk
- 1 tablespoon vanilla
- ⅛ teaspoon salt
- 8–10 cups powdered sugar

Blend the cream cheese, milk, vanilla, and salt. Gradually add the sugar, beating until frosting is smooth and has a spreading consistency. If necessary, stir in additional milk, 1 tablespoon at a time.

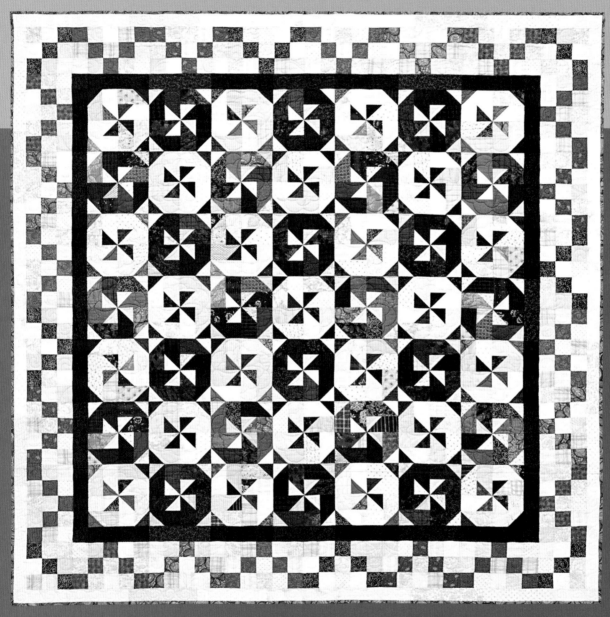

Not Just Huckleberry Pie *quilt*

To honor the huckleberry's color—but add a little creativity—I chose to work with analogous colors, which are next to each other on the color wheel: blue, blue-violet, purple, and red-violet. The Berry blocks are made from Half-Square triangles! See how surprisingly easy they are to make. Sew, eat, and enjoy!

CUTTING

From each fabric

From each ¼ yard, cut 1 strip 6″ × 42″.

- From the purple strips, cut a total of 12 squares 6″ × 6″.

- From the red-violet strips, cut a total of 12 squares 6″ × 6″.

- From the blue strips, cut a total of 16 squares 6″ × 6″.

- From the blue-violet strips, cut a total of 16 squares 6″ × 6″.

- From the light strips, cut a total of 56 squares 6″ × 6″.

From the remainder of each strip, cut 2 strips 2¾″ wide (lengths will vary). Cut a total of 132 squares 2¾″. These strips and squares will be used in the border.

Draw a diagonal line on the wrong side of the light 6″ squares only.

Draw a diagonal line.

Berry Block Color Key

BLUE
Berry Blocks
Light Pinwheel

BLUE-VIOLET
Berry Blocks
Light Pinwheel

RED-VIOLET
Berry Blocks
Light Pinwheel

PURPLE
Berry Blocks
Light Pinwheel

BLUE
Berry Blocks
Blue Pinwheel

BLUE-VIOLET
Berry Blocks
Blue-Violet Pinwheel

RED-VIOLET
Berry Blocks
Red-Violet Pinwheel

PURPLE
Berry Blocks
Purple Pinwheel

QUILTED BY: Carrie Peterson
FINISHED QUILT SIZE: 86″ × 86″

YARDAGE

- ⅓ yard each of 8 different blue prints, plaids, and stripes

- ¼ yard each of 8 different blue-violet (periwinkle) prints, plaids, and stripes

- ¼ yard each of 8 different purple prints, plaids, and stripes

- ¼ yard each of 8 different red-violet prints, plaids, and stripes

- ¼ yard each of 32 different light cream, off-white, light tan, or muslin prints, plaids, and stripes. Keep the lights very light. They are very light in the real quilt.

- Backing fabric: 7⅔ yards (2 horizontal seams)

- Binding fabric: ¾ yard of 1 red-violet or purple fabric

- Batting: 92″ × 92″

CONSTRUCTION

Make sure your ¼″ seam allowance is accurate—all blocks assume an accurate ¼″ seam.

MAKING HALF-SQUARE TRIANGLES

1. Pair 1 colored square with 1 light square, right sides together. Refer to pages 7–8 for Half-Square triangle construction Steps 1–4.

2. Press the seam toward the colored fabric. Each pair of squares yields 2 Half-Square triangles. Make a total of 112 Half-Square triangles, 24 purple, 24 red-violet, 32 blue, and 32 blue-violet.

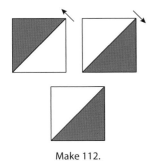

Make 112.

3. Trim all Half-Square triangles to 5½″ × 5½″.

MAKING BERRY BLOCKS

When making Berry blocks for this quilt, use an assortment of fabrics from the same color family. Do not mix colors. For example, when making blue blocks, use only blue; do not combine with purple pieces.

1. Sort the Half-Square triangles into 2 identical piles so that half of the Half-Square triangles of each color fabric are in the first pile and half of the Half-Square triangles of the same color fabric are in the second pile. For example, 16 of the blue-violet Half-Square triangles will be in the first pile, and 16 will be in the second pile. Repeat with all the Half-Square triangles. You will have 56 Half-Square triangles in each pile. Stack all the Half-Square triangles in the first pile so that the colored triangle is in the top left of the Half-Square triangle block. In the second pile, stack them so that the colored triangle is in the bottom left of the Half-Square triangle block.

2. Cut in half vertically to form rectangles 2¾″ wide × 5½″ long.

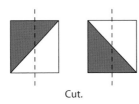

Cut.

3. From the bottom edge of all the rectangles, cut off ½″. Be careful: do not cut ½″ off the edge that includes a triangle. Cut off the edge that does not have a triangle on it.

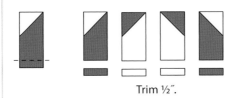

Trim ½″.

4. Sew 2 rectangles (with small light triangles). Do not mix colors. Make 24 purple units, 24 red-violet units, 32 blue-violet units, and 32 blue units. Make a total of 112 units.

Make 112.

5. Sew 2 rectangles (with small colored triangles). Do not mix colors. Make 24 purple units, 24 red-violet units, 32 blue-violet units, and 32 blue units. Make a total of 112 units.

Make 112.

6. Combine 4 units of the same color to make the Berry blocks; occasionally you will need to repeat a fabric in the same block. Make 28 Berry blocks that are light with a colored pinwheel center and background and 28 Berry blocks that are dark with a light pinwheel center and background. You need 49 Berry blocks; there will be 7 blocks left over.

 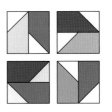

Make 28.

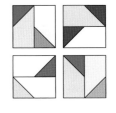

Make 28.

ASSEMBLING THE QUILT TOP

1. Refer to the photo on page 52 and the Quilt Assembly Diagram on page 56. Arrange the Berry blocks, alternating light and dark Berry blocks. Notice that I arranged 4 vertical rows with blue-violet and blue Berry blocks, 3 vertical rows with purple and red-violet Berry blocks, and light Berry blocks in all 4 corners.

2. Sew together in horizontal rows. Press seams in opposite directions from row to row. Sew the rows together. Press as desired.

ADDING THE BORDERS

When sewing borders to a quilt top, mark the quilt and each border piece as follows: Fold the quilt and border pieces to find the midpoints, and mark with pins. Then find the quarter points, and mark with pins. With right sides together, match midpoints, quarter points, and ends prior to sewing pieces together.

FIRST BORDER

1. The first border is purple and red-violet. Cut 16 red-violet 2¾″ × 9½″ rectangles, 12 purple 2¾″ × 9½″ rectangles, and 4 purple 2¾″ squares from the leftover purple and red-violet strips. Sew 7 rectangles together end-to-end. Start with a red-violet rectangle, alternate red-violet and purple rectangles, and end with a red-violet rectangle. Make 4. Press as desired.

2. Sew the border strips to the sides of the quilt top. Press seams toward the borders.

3. Sew a 2¾˝ purple square to opposite ends of the remaining 2 first border strips. Press. Sew the top and bottom borders to the quilt top. Press seams toward the borders.

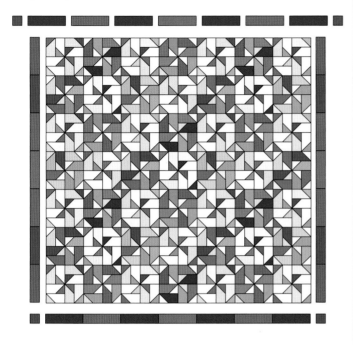

SECOND BORDER

1. The second border is blue, blue-violet, and light, which creates a scallop. Choose 3 leftover blue fabrics and 3 leftover blue-violet fabric strips 2¾˝ wide. Cut from your extra blue and blue-violet fabrics an identical strip of each fabric you have chosen 2¾˝ × 42˝. You will now have 2 strips of each fabric, but 1 will be less than 42˝ long.

2. Light fabrics can be an assortment of 2¾˝ strips that you have already cut. They will be less than 42˝ long.

3. Also cut 132 light squares from your leftover light fabrics, 2¾˝ × 2¾˝. You need these in both the scallop blocks and the corner blocks.

4. Pair 1 blue and 1 light strip. If 1 is longer than the other (and it probably will be), add another strip and continue sewing until you have sewn all of the same blue fabric to light strips. Press toward the blue fabric.

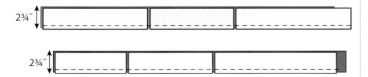

5. Cut 20 sections 2¾˝ wide. The blue fabric will be the same in all the sections, but the light fabrics will vary.

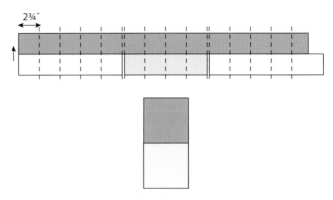

Make 20 of each
Blue or Blue-Violet/Light combination.

6. Arrange 5 sections and 5 light squares 2¾˝ × 2¾˝. Sew together in rows. Press seams in opposite directions from row to row. Sew the rows together. Make 4 blocks with the same blue fabric. Light fabrics will vary. Repeat with each blue and blue-violet fabric. Make a total of 24 blocks.

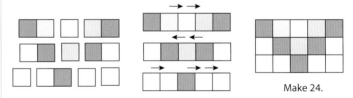

Make 24.

CORNER BLOCKS

1. Choose 1 blue-violet fabric strip 2¾˝ wide. You may need to cut an identical fabric strip from your leftover fabric 2¾˝ × 42˝. Light fabrics can be an assortment of 2¾˝ fabric strips you have already cut. They will be less than 42˝ long.

2. Sew 1 blue-violet and 1 light strip together. Press toward the blue-violet fabric. Cut 12 sections 2¾˝ wide. If necessary, sew a second blue-violet and light strip so you have enough sections.

3. Arrange 3 sections and 3 light squares. Sew together in rows. Press in opposite directions from row to row. Sew the rows together.

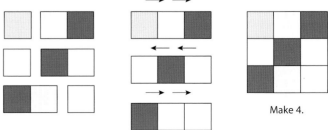

Make 4.

ASSEMBLING THE SECOND BORDER

1. Refer to the Quilt Assembly Diagram, below, and arrange 6 blue and blue-violet blocks as shown, alternating the colors. Sew them together to make a border strip. Repeat with the remaining blue and blue-violet blocks to make a total of 4 border strips.

2. Sew 2 of the border strips to opposite sides of the quilt top. Notice how the border strip is placed to form scallops. Press the seams toward the first border.

3. Sew the corner blocks to opposite ends of the remaining 2 border strips. Note the placement of both the corner blocks and the border strips. Press seams as desired. Sew these border strips to the top and bottom of the quilt. Press seams toward the first border.

THIRD BORDER

1. The third border uses lights only. Sew together light strips, 2¾" wide and of varying lengths, end-to-end to create 1 strip approximately 340" long. Press seams as desired. From this long strip, cut 2 strips 81½" long and 2 strips 86" long.

2. Sew the 81½" strips to opposite sides of the quilt. Press seams toward the third border. Sew the 86" long strips to the top and bottom of the quilt. Press seams toward the third border.

3. Layer the top with batting and backing. Quilt and bind as desired.

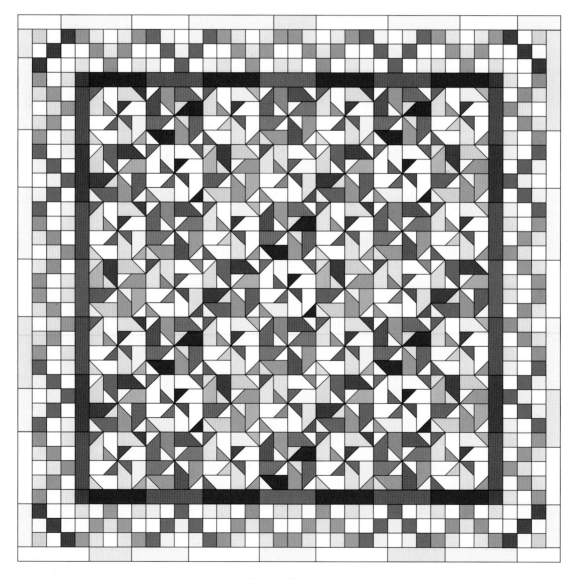

Quilt Assembly Diagram

Berry Charming
by Suzanne Barsness.
Quilted by Carrie Peterson.
38˝ × 45˝.

Cranberry Chutney
by Penny A. Hazelton.
Quilted by Sue Lohse.
85˝ × 92˝.

NOT JUST HUCKLEBERRY PIE QUILT   **57**

Gooseberry Pie
by Suzanne Barsness.
Quilted by Carrie Peterson.
71″ × 71″.

Rhapsody in Blue(berries)
by Joan Christ.
Quilted by Carrie Peterson.
59″ × 71″.

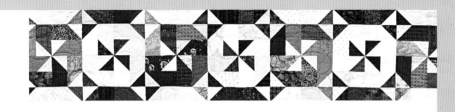

Not Just Huckleberry Pie

Not Just Huckleberry Pie includes more than huckleberries! This scrumptious pie includes apples, too.
And if you can't find huckleberries, blueberries are a good substitute.

INGREDIENTS

- ¾ cup sugar
- ¼ cup flour
- ½ teaspoon nutmeg
- ½ teaspoon cinnamon
- 6 cups Granny Smith apples (about 4 apples), peeled, cored, and thinly sliced
- 2 cups huckleberries or blueberries (fresh or frozen)
- 1 pie crust, 9″, unbaked (and thawed, if frozen)
- Vanilla or huckleberry ice cream

CRUMBLY TOPPING

- 1 cup flour
- ¾ cup butter, cut into pieces
- 1 cup brown sugar

1. Combine sugar, flour, nutmeg, cinnamon, apple slices, and berries.
Place in pie crust. Combine topping ingredients. Mix until crumbly. Sprinkle over fruit.

2. Bake at 375° for 50 minutes. Cover with foil for the last 10 minutes if the top browns too quickly.
Test with a knife for doneness. If apples are slightly firm, they will soften as the pie cools.

3. Serve warm or cold with vanilla ice cream or huckleberry ice cream.

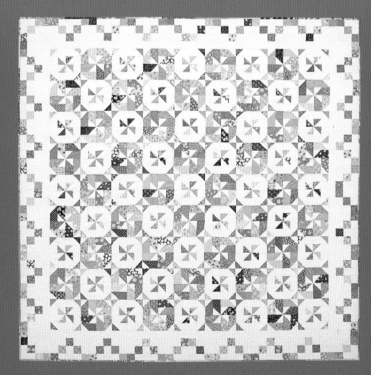

Baking from Scratch the Old Fashioned Way
by Cate Franklin.
Quilted by Helene Kempf.
96″ × 96″.

It's a Mystery
Dessert *quilt*

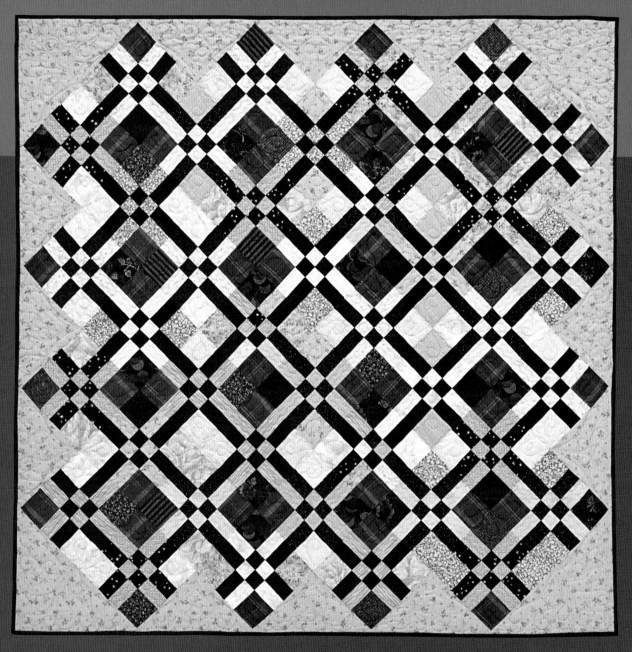

 his quilt's colors were inspired by an idea from one of my students. It was suggested that I choose colors for a quilt, and then have students choose one color of their choice, a "mystery" color, to add. My chosen colors are black, gray, and red. My mystery color is blue. Choose your own mystery color, and have fun.

CUTTING

Black fabric

- From each of the 5 black fabrics, cut 4 strips 2″ × 42″.

Red fabric

- From each of the 6 red fabrics, cut 1 strip 3½″ × 42″.

From each strip, cut 7 squares 3½″ × 3½″ for a total of 42 squares. You will use 40.

Mystery fabric

- From the mystery fabric, cut 4 strips 3½″ × 42″.

From these strips, cut 40 squares 3½″ × 3½″.

Gray fabric

- From each of the 13 gray fabrics, cut 2 strips 2″ × 42″ and 1 strip 3½″ × 42″.

From each 3½″-wide strip, cut 7 squares 3½″ × 3½″ for a total of 91 squares. You will use 80.

- From the side and corner triangle gray fabric, cut 5 squares 15½″ × 15½″.

Cut 3 of these squares on both diagonals to yield 4 triangles per square for a total of 12 triangles. These will be your side triangles.

Cut the remaining 2 squares in half diagonally to yield 2 triangles per square for a total of 4 triangles. These will be your corner triangles.

QUILTED BY: Carrie Peterson
FINISHED QUILT SIZE: 65¼″ × 65¼″

YARDAGE

- If you plan on adding borders, you will need the yardage in parentheses.

Block Fabrics

- ⅓ yard each (½ yard each including borders) of 13 light and medium-light gray fabrics
- ¼ yard each (¼ yard each including borders) of 6 medium red fabrics
- ⅓ yard each (½ yard each including borders) of 5 dark black fabrics
- ½ yard (⅝ yard including borders) of 1 mystery fabric, medium in value

Side and Corner Triangles

- 1½ yards of 1 light or medium-light gray fabric

- Borders: Optional
- Backing fabric: 4 yards (more if you add borders)
- Binding fabric: ⅝ yard (more if you add borders)
- Batting: 71″ × 71″ (more if you add borders)

Note

Your gray fabrics should read gray, not black and white, from a distance. Your gray fabrics should also read light or medium-light, but not medium or dark. Your black fabrics should read dark from a distance. Sometimes black fabrics read medium if they have lighter designs on them. Be careful. For your mystery fabric, choose a medium value in your choice of color. A light mystery fabric would blend with the grays. A dark mystery fabric might read too dark and not be distinguishable from the black fabrics.

CONSTRUCTION

Make sure your ¼″ seam allowance is accurate—all blocks assume an accurate ¼″ seam.

MAKING THE BLOCKS

Use 20 of the 2″-wide black strips and 20 of the 2″-wide assorted gray fabrics to make 160 Strip blocks and 40 Four-Patch blocks.

Color Code

 = Light Grays

 = Mystery Color

 = Red

 = Black

1. Pair 1 black strip and 1 gray strip, right sides together. Sew strips together.

Sew strips together.

2. Press seams toward the black fabric. Cut into 8 sections, each 3½″ wide.

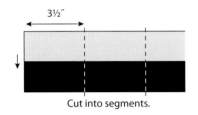

Cut into segments.

Strip block

3. From the remaining strip, cut 4 sections, each 2″ wide.

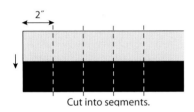

Cut into segments.

4. Sew together 2 sections, 2″ wide. Press as desired. Make 2 Four-Patch blocks.

Sew into Four-patch block. Make 2.

5. Arrange 4 Strip blocks, 1 Four-Patch block, 1 red 3½″ square, and 1 mystery 3½″ square.

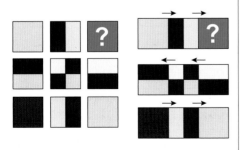

6. Sew together in rows. Press seams in opposite directions from row to row. Make 2.

7. Repeat Steps 1–5 with the remaining 19 black 2″-wide strips, 19 gray 2″-wide strips (you will have 6 left over), 38 red 3½″ squares, and 38 mystery 3½″ squares to make a total of 40 blocks.

Make 40.

ASSEMBLING THE QUILT TOP

1. Arrange the blocks and side triangles as shown. Play with the arrangement until you are satisfied.

2. Sew the blocks and side triangles together in diagonal rows. (You won't be adding triangles to the 2 middle rows.) Press seams in opposite directions from row to row. Trim the points created by the side triangles so that the top of the side triangles are flat, are not pointed, and line up with the edge of the blocks.

3. Sew the rows together. Press.

4. Sew corner triangles last. Press seams toward the corner triangles.

5. Trim edges ¾″ from the points of the blocks.

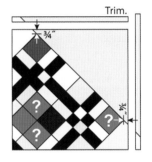

6. Layer the top with batting and backing. Quilt and bind as desired.

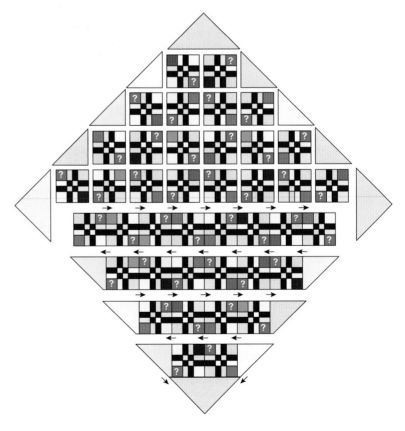

Quilt Assembly Diagram

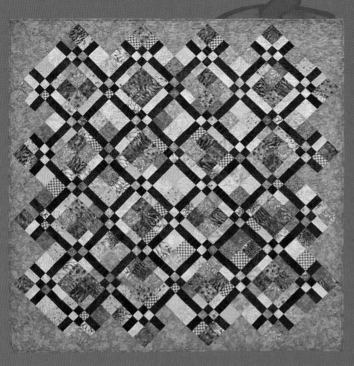

Soothing Mystery by Suzanne Barsness.
Quilted by Carrie Peterson. 64″ × 64″.

The Wedding Quilt by Dorothy Finley.
Quilted by Carrie Peterson. 63″ × 63″.

Butter Cookies by Rachel Barsness.
Quilted by Carrie Peterson. 61″ × 74″.

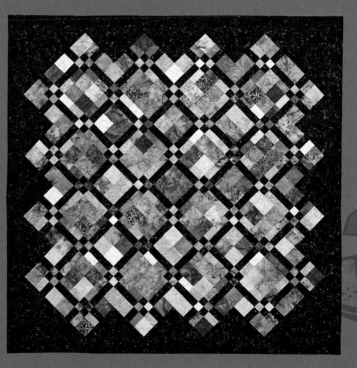

Untitled by Merry Maricich.
Quilted by Peggy Wilbur. 69″ × 69″.

Mystery Dessert: *Individual Baked Alaska*

INGREDIENTS

- 3″ fudge brownie square (or 3″ cookie) for base
- Vanilla ice cream (or your choice of flavor)
- Meringue
- Homemade hot fudge sauce (could be purchased)
- 3 eggs
- 1 teaspoon real vanilla extract
- ¾ cup cocoa
- ¼ cup vegetable oil
- 1 cup flour
- ½ teaspoon salt

FUDGY BROWNIES

- 1 cup butter
- 2 cups sugar

1. Cream ½ cup of butter with sugar. Add eggs and beat until light and fluffy. Add vanilla. Set aside.

2. Using a whisk, mix cocoa and oil, then, on low heat, melt remaining butter with this mixture. Cool. Beat into first mixture. Add flour and salt. Mix well and pour into greased and floured pan (9″ × 13″). Bake in 350° oven 25–30 minutes (test with a toothpick). Cool. Cut into 3″ squares.

Ice Cream

- Place 8 scoops of ice cream onto a baking sheet and freeze until firm.

Homemade Hot Fudge Sauce

- ¾ cup unsweetened cocoa
- ¼ cup vegetable oil
- 1 cup milk
- ¼ teaspoon salt
- 2 cups white sugar
- ¼ cup light corn syrup
- 2 tablespoons butter (not margarine)
- ½ teaspoon real vanilla extract

1. In a saucepan, whisk together the cocoa and oil. Add milk. Stir (with a whisk) until smooth.

2. Heat over medium-high heat, stirring constantly. Add salt, sugar, and corn syrup. Boil for 5 minutes. Remove from heat, and add butter and vanilla.

Meringue

- 4 egg whites at room temperature
- ½ teaspoon cream of tartar
- ⅛ teaspoon salt
- ½ cup sugar, added 1 tablespoon at a time
- 1 teaspoon real vanilla extract or almond flavoring

1. Beat egg whites, cream of tartar, and salt until foamy.

2. Slowly, add sugar, 1 tablespoon at a time. Continue beating until stiff peaks form.

3. Add vanilla or almond flavoring.

Assembling the Dessert

1. To assemble individual Baked Alaskas, place the ice cream on the brownie square (or cookie) and press to secure. Quickly spread the meringue over the ice cream and cookie, covering completely. Swirl the meringue, or simply form peaks overall by pressing the back of the spoon into the meringue surface and pulling away quickly.

2. Put the individual desserts into the freezer until ready to serve. They can be made 24 hours in advance and frozen.

3. To bake, preheat the oven to 475°. Place the desserts on a cookie sheet. Bake for 2 minutes or until peaks are lightly brown. Serve with home-made (or purchased) hot fudge sauce on top.

Valentine Cookies *quilt*

In My Heart You Are All Stars

his quilt is dedicated to my students in my dessert quilt classes. They are a wonderful group of loyal quilters, many of whom had their quilts in my first book about dessert quilts, *Sweet Treats*. In my heart they really are all stars. They make beautiful quilts, stretch my ideas, change my colors, and in general do very little that I tell them to do—so I learn so much from them, and I love them all.

YARDAGE

- ½ yard of 10 different rich, bright-red fabrics (medium in value, not light or dark)

- ½ yard of 10 different rich, bright-fuchsia fabrics (medium in value, not light or dark)

- ½ yard of 10 different medium-dark or dark black fabrics

Again, because this is important, make sure the red fabrics are rich and bright, not light or dark. Make sure the fuchsia fabrics are rich and bright, not light or dark. The black fabrics should read dark or medium-dark, not lighter than that. The blacks should be the darkest fabrics in this quilt.

- Backing fabric: 5 yards*

  *If fabric is less than 44" you will need 7⅓ yards (2 horizontal seams).

- Binding fabric: ¾ yard

- Batting: 87" × 87"

Color Code

 = Fucshsia

 = Red

 = Black

CUTTING

- From each ½ yard, cut 1 strip 4½" × 42".

- From each fabric, cut 4 squares 4½" × 4½" and 5 squares 3½" × 3½".

- From each fabric, cut 2 squares 10½" × 10½".

- Cut 1 additional fuchsia square 10½" × 10½".

> ## Note
> I used 12 different red fabrics, 12 different fuchsia fabrics, and 12 different black fabrics. Mathematically, you will have enough fabric to complete the quilt top with 10 of each. I used 12 because although I had more fabric leftovers, this gave me the flexibility to use my best blocks and leave out the ones that didn't have enough contrast. It also gave the quilt a greater variety of fabrics (36 as opposed to 30).

CONSTRUCTION

Make sure your ¼" seam allowance is accurate—all blocks assume an accurate ¼" seam.

Star Blocks
MAKING HALF-SQUARE TRIANGLES

1. Choose 16 black and 16 red 4½" squares. Pair 1 black square and 1 red square, right sides together. Refer to pages 7–8 for Half-Square triangle construction Steps 1–4.

2. Each pair of squares yields 2 Half-Square triangles. Using the same 2 fabrics, repeat to make 2 more identical Half-Square triangles. You should have 4 Half-Square triangles that are identical.

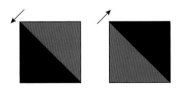

3. Repeat with the remaining black and remaining red squares. Make a total of 32 black/red Half-Square triangles (8 sets of 4 identical ones). Do not trim.

Make 32 total
red/black.

4. Choose 18 fuchsia and 18 red 4½˝ squares, making sure you have contrast from a distance. Repeat Steps 1 and 2 to make a total of 36 Half-Square triangles (9 sets of 4 identical ones). Do not trim.

Make 36 total
fuchsia/red.

5. Choose 16 fuchsia and 16 black 4½˝ squares. Repeat Steps 1 and 2 to make a total of 32 Half-Square triangles (8 sets of 4 identical ones). Do not trim.

Make 32 total
black/fuchsia.

MAKING THE STAR POINTS (QUARTER-SQUARE TRIANGLES)

Note: When making the Star Points and Hour Glass Blocks, refer to the Quarter-Square Triangle instructions on pages 45–46.

1. Combine 2 Half-Square triangles with identical fabrics to make Quarter-Square triangles. Pair 2 identical Half-Square triangles, right sides together. Fold back 1 Half-Square triangle to confirm that the same colors and fabrics are opposite each other.

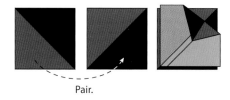

Pair.

2. Pair 32 black/red Half-Square triangles to make 32 black/red Quarter-Square triangles.

Make 32 total
red/black.

3. Pair 36 fuchsia/red Half-Square triangles to make 36 fuchsia/red Quarter-Square triangles.

Make 36 total
fuchsia/red.

4. Pair 32 black/fuchsia Half-Square triangles to make 32 black/fuchsia Quarter-Square triangles.

Make 32 total
black/fuchsia.

5. Trim all Quarter-Square triangles to 3½˝ × 3½˝ (refer to Steps 2, 3 and 4 on page 46—your half block measurement is 1¾˝). You will have a total of 100 Quarter-Square triangles. You need all 100.

6. Combine 4 identical fuchsia/red Quarter-Square triangles, 1 fuchsia 3½˝ square, and 4 identical red 3½˝ squares. Sew together in rows. Press seams away from the Quarter-Square triangles in all 3 rows. Sew the rows together. Press seams as desired. Make 9.

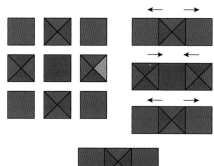

Make 9 total
fuchsia Star blocks.

7. Combine 4 identical red/black Quarter-Square triangles, 1 red 3½˝ square, and 4 identical black 3½˝ squares. Sew together in rows. Press seams away from the Quarter-Square triangles in all 3 rows. Sew the rows together. Press seams as desired. Make 8.

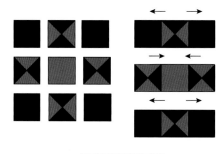

Make 8 total
red Star blocks.

8. Combine 4 identical black/fuchsia Quarter-Square triangles, 1 black 3½˝ square, and 4 identical fuchsia 3½˝ squares. Sew together in rows. Press seams away from the Quarter-Square triangles in all 3 rows. Sew the rows together. Press seams as desired. Make 8.

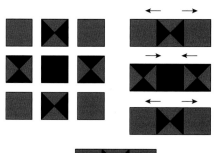

Make 8 total
black Star blocks.

HOURGLASS BLOCKS

(LARGE QUARTER-SQUARE TRIANGLES
BETWEEN THE STAR BLOCKS AND ON
THE BORDER)

1. Choose 9 black and 9 fuchsia 10½″
squares. Pair 1 black square and 1 fuchsia
square, right sides together. Refer to
pages 45–46 for Quarter-Square triangle
construction Steps 1–4.

2. Repeat with the remaining black and
remaining fuchsia squares. Make a total
of 18 black/fuchsia Half-Square triangles.
Do not trim.

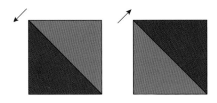

Make 18 total
black/fuchsia.

3. Choose 8 red and 8 black 10½″
squares. Repeat Steps 1 and 2 to make
a total of 16 red/black Half-Square triangles. Do not trim.

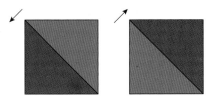

Make 16 total
red/black.

4. Choose 12 red and 12 fuchsia 10½″
squares, making sure you have contrast
from a distance. Repeat Step 1 to make a
total of 24 Half-Square triangles (9 sets of
4 identical ones). Do not trim.

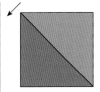

Make 24 total
red/fuchsia.

COMPLETING THE HOURGLASS BLOCKS

1. Combine 2 Half-Square triangles to
make Quarter-Square triangles. Note the
placement of colors. It is different than
for the smaller Quarter-Square triangles
for the Star blocks. These are black next
to black, red next to red, fuchsia next to
fuchsia. Like colors will be next to each
other, not across from each other.

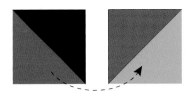

Pair.

2. Pair 2 fuchsia/black Half-Square triangles, right sides together. Fold back
1 Half-Square triangle to confirm that
the same colors are next to each other.
Black should be next to black and fuchsia
next to fuchsia. Refer to pages 45–46
for Quarter-Square triangle construction
Steps 1–4.

3. Each pair of Half-Square triangles
yields 2 Quarter-Square triangles
(Hourglass blocks). Make a total of 18
fuchsia/black Quarter-Square triangles.

Make 18 total
fuchsia/black.

4. Repeat Step 1 using red/black Half-
Square triangles to make a total of 16
red/black Quarter-Square triangles.

Make 16 total
red/black

5. Repeat Step 1 using red/fuchsia Half-
Square triangles to make a total of
24 red/fuchsia Quarter-Square triangles.

Make 24 total
red/fuchsia.

6. Trim all Quarter-Square triangles to
9½″ × 9½″. You will have a total of 58
Quarter-Square triangles. You need 56.

---

hint

Very important: Before you sew the quilt top together, step back and view your final border arrangement from
a distance. Make sure you really see how the Hourglass blocks on the border read. Not all your Hourglass blocks
will have the contrast you want. Use them anyway unless you have created extra Hourglass blocks because you
used more than 10 fabrics of each color in the beginning. As long as most of the Hourglass blocks have good
contrast, the viewer's eye will "fill in" where the contrast isn't as noticeable.

PATCHWORK PARTY

Notice the arrangement of the blocks. Start in the upper left corner and proceed diagonally to the lower right corner: fuchsia Star block with red background, red/black Hourglass blocks, red Stars with black background, black/fuchsia Hourglass blocks, black Stars with fuchsia background, fuchsia/red Hourglass blocks; then repeat: fuchsia Star blocks with red background, and so forth. The background color becomes the color of the Star in the next diagonal row.

Very important: Substitute different Hourglass blocks (in the correct colors) as needed to get the best contrast when creating diagonal rows. Step back and view your final block arrangement from a distance. Rearrange and/or substitute blocks as needed until block placement is pleasing, identical fabrics aren't next to each other most of the time, and contrast is good (not perfect).

ARRANGING THE BLOCKS

1. Using all 25 Star blocks, 8 red/black Hourglass blocks, 8 fuchsia/black Hourglass blocks, and 8 fuchsia/red Hourglass blocks, arrange the blocks for the quilt Center as shown in the Quilt Assembly Diagram, right.

2. Arrange the remaining 32 Hourglass blocks on all 4 sides of the quilt top to create a sawtooth border. Notice that the lighter half of the Hourglass blocks are next to the quilt top, with the points all pointing in the same direction. For the 4 Hourglass blocks in the corners, turn them as desired, paying more attention to value than color.

3. Once you have viewed your entire quilt from a distance and are satisfied with the placement of your blocks, sew blocks in each horizontal row together. Press seams in opposite directions from row to row.

4. Sew rows together. Press as desired.

5. Layer the top with batting and backing. Quilt and bind as desired.

Quilt Assembly Diagram

Road to Market
by Ann Elizabeth Rindge.
80″ × 80″.

Almost a Valentine Cookie
by Joseph Pepia.
Quilted by Heather Rogers.
80″ × 80″.

Valentine Cookies with Creamy Frosting

COOKIES

- 2 cups sugar
- 1 cup butter, softened to room temperature
- 1 cup sour cream
- 2 eggs
- 1 teaspoon baking soda
- 1 teaspoon real vanilla extract
- 7 cups flour

1. Combine all of the ingredients. Add additional flour if the dough is sticky. But if you add additional flour (I didn't), don't add too much. You will add additional flour to the dough when it is rolled out on a floured surface.

2. Roll dough out on a lightly floured surface to about ¼˝ thick. Cut out with a heart-shaped cookie cutter. Carefully place hearts on a lightly greased baking sheet.

3. Bake at 350° for approximately 10 minutes or until cookies are just slightly brown on the edges. The cookies should be light, almost white. Do not overbake unless you like crisp cookies. Makes 6–7 dozen medium-sized heart cookies.

CREAMY FROSTING

- 4 cups powdered sugar
- ½ cup butter
- 1½ teaspoons vanilla
- ¼ cup milk plus additional tablespoons as needed
- Red and pink sprinkles and Red Hots

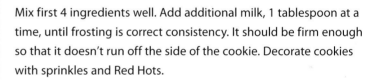

Mix first 4 ingredients well. Add additional milk, 1 tablespoon at a time, until frosting is correct consistency. It should be firm enough so that it doesn't run off the side of the cookie. Decorate cookies with sprinkles and Red Hots.

Enjoy!

Note

The amount of frosting doesn't look like it is enough for all the cookies, but it is. However, if you are very generous with the amount of frosting you put on each cookie, you might need to make a little more frosting.

Martha Washington Cake *quilt*

T his quilt was designed for the Quilter's Unlimited Quilt Show in Chantilly, Virginia, near Washington, D.C. It honors our very first First Lady, Martha Washington, and is based on the cake she served her guests during the holidays. This quilt features a Martha Washington Star block in the center and Cake Stand Basket blocks, set in a very traditional medallion style.

The focus of this quilt is refining the concept of value. In this quilt there are five values, not the usual three. The five values are light, medium-light, medium, medium-dark, and dark. The colors chosen to represent these values are cream, off-white, muslin, tan, and beige for the lights; golds for the medium-lights; reds for the mediums; blue for the medium-darks; and black for the darks. If you change the colors, keep in mind the values so that you will have contrast in your quilt.

CUTTING

In this pattern, I have referred to light fabrics as "lights" (not just 1 light fabric), red fabrics as "reds" (not just 1 red), and the same with blues, blacks, and golds. When you see these words, unless otherwise noted, choose a variety of different fabrics in the color specified. Exceptions are the Basket blocks and the Martha Washington Star. The Basket blocks aren't made with a variety of lights and reds. The light is the same and the red is the same in each Basket block. The Martha Washington Star isn't made with a variety of lights, reds, and blacks. The red is the same, and there are 2 different lights that are the same but in different places in the block. There are 3 different blacks that are the same but in different places in the block.

Martha Washington Star block, cut

- 2 same black squares, 2″ × 2″
- 2 same light squares, 2″ × 2″
- 2 same red squares, 2½″ × 2½″
- 2 same black squares, 3″ × 3″
- 4 same black rectangles, 2½″ × 4½″, and 4 same black squares, 2½″ × 2½″
- 8 same light squares, 2½″ × 2½″

Blue, gold, and black section around the Star, cut

- 16 blue rectangles, 2½″ × 4½″
- 28 gold squares, 2½″ × 2½″
- 4 black rectangles, 2½″ × 4½″

Red border, cut

- 4 red rectangles, 2½″ × 16½″
- 4 light squares, 2½″ × 2½″

Zigzag border, cut

- 44 black rectangles, 2½″ × 4½″
- 88 gold squares, 2½″ × 2½″
- 4 light squares, 2½″ × 2½″
- 4 red squares, 2½″ × 2½″

Look-Like-But-Aren't-Four-Patches border, cut

- 7 gold strips, 2½″ × 42″
- 7 black strips, 2½″ × 42″
- 4 blue strips, 2½″ × 28½″

Cake Stand Basket blocks, for each Basket, cut

- 1 light square, 7″ × 7″
- 1 red square, 7″ × 7″
- 8 light squares, 2½″ × 2½″
- 10 red squares, 2½″ × 2½″
- 2 red rectangles, 2½″ × 6½″

Note that lights are the same fabric and reds are the same fabric in each Basket.

- Cut 3 additional lights and 3 additional reds to make 3 more Baskets. You will make a total of 4 Baskets.

For the outside border, cut

- 48 blue squares, 4½″ × 4½″
- 4 light squares, 4½″ × 4½″
- 96 light squares, 2½″ × 2½″

QUILTED BY: Carrie Peterson
FINISHED QUILT SIZE: 56½″ × 56½″

YARDAGE

- ½ yard each of 5 different fabrics: light cream, off-white, tan, muslin, and beige
- ½ yard each of 5 different medium-light gold fabrics
- ½ yard each of 5 different medium red fabrics
- ½ yard each of 5 different medium-dark blue fabrics
- ½ yard each of 5 different dark black fabrics
- Backing fabric: 3½ yards
- Binding fabric: ⅝ yard of medium-dark blue fabric or your choice
- Batting: 62″ × 62″

Color Code

	= Light
	= Gold
	= Blue
	= Red
	= Black

CONSTRUCTION

Make sure your ¼" seam allowance is accurate—all blocks assume an accurate ¼" seam.

MAKING THE MARTHA WASHINGTON STAR

1. Pair 1 black 2" square with 1 light 2" square, right sides together. Refer to pages 7–8 for Half-Square triangle construction Steps 1–4.

2. Repeat with the other black and the other light 2" squares. Make a total of 4 Half-Square triangles. Trim to 1½" × 1½".

Make 4 total.

3. Sew these Half-Square triangles together to make a Pinwheel. Press seams open.

4. Cut the 2 red 2½" × 2½" squares on the diagonal to get 4 triangles. With right sides together, center 2 triangles on opposite sides of the Pinwheel block. Note that the center seam of the Pinwheel allows you to center the point of the triangle exactly.

5. Pin to keep the triangle from shifting as you sew. Sew the 2 triangles to opposite sides of the Pinwheel block. Press seams toward the triangles. Trim the ends that stick out past the edge of the Pinwheel block.

6. Sew the remaining 2 red triangles to the remaining sides of the Pinwheel block. Press seams toward the triangles. Trim this block to 3¼" × 3¼".

7. Cut the 2 black 3" × 3" squares on the diagonal to get 4 triangles. Repeat Steps 4–6 to sew black triangles to the Pinwheel block. Trim this block to 4½" × 4½".

8. To make the Star points, mark the diagonal on the wrong side of the 2½" light squares. Place 1 light 2½" square on 1 edge of 1 black 2½" × 4½" rectangle, right sides together. Sew on the diagonal line. Press; square up the edge of the flipped light fabric to match the edge of the black fabric, if necessary; then trim out the back 2 layers of fabric.

Draw a diagonal line.

Stitch on line.   Press and trim.

9. Place another 2½" light square to the other edge of the black rectangle. Sew on the diagonal line. Press; square up the edge, if necessary; and trim back 2 layers of fabric. This unit becomes 2 of the Star's points.

Press and trim.

10. Repeat Steps 8 and 9 to sew the remaining black rectangles and 2½" light squares together to make 4 Star point units.

11. Sew 2 Star point units to opposite sides of the center Pinwheel block. Press seams open.

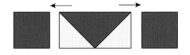

12. To complete the Star, sew 2 black 2½" squares to opposite ends of the 2 remaining Star point units. Press toward the squares. Make 2.

13. Sew the rows together. Press.

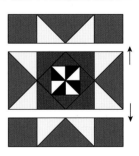

BLUE, GOLD, AND BLACK SECTION AROUND THE STAR

1. Mark the diagonal on the wrong side of 20 of the gold squares.

Draw a diagonal line.

2. Place 1 gold square and 1 blue rectangle right sides together. Sew on the diagonal line. Press; square up the edge of the flipped gold fabric to match the edge of the blue fabric, if necessary; then trim out the back 2 layers of fabric. Make 8. *Note: You will have extra blue rectangles.*

Draw diagonal line.　Stitch on line.　Press and trim.

Make 8 total.

3. Repeat Step 2 to sew and flip 1 gold square to 1 blue rectangle. Note that the triangle direction is different. Make 4. You will have extra blue rectangles.

Draw diagonal line.　Stitch on line.　Press and trim.

Make 4 total.

4. Repeat the sew-and-flip method to sew 8 gold squares to the edges of 4 black rectangles. These units look like the Star points, but they're gold and black and won't be used as points on a Star. Make 4.

Make 4
total.

5. Arrange the units from Steps 2, 3, and 4; the remaining blue rectangles; and the remaining gold squares around the Martha Washington Star block.

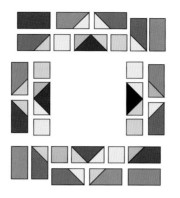

6. Sew units together in sections. Press seams as desired. Sew 2 shorter sections to the sides of the Star section. Press. Sew the larger sections to the Star section. Press.

RED BORDER

1. Sew 2 red rectangles to opposite sides of the center section. Press seams toward the red rectangle border.

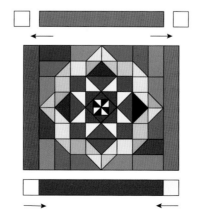

2. Sew the remaining 2 red rectangles to 4 light squares. Press seams toward the red rectangles. Sew these units to the top and bottom of the Star section. Press the seams toward the border.

ZIGZAG BORDER

1. Mark a diagonal line on the wrong side of 88 gold squares. Sew gold squares to black rectangles using the sew-and-flip method to sew, flip, press, and trim. Make 44.

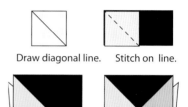

Draw diagonal line.　Stitch on line.

Press and trim.
Make 44 total.

2. Arrange and sew 5 units together as shown. Press. Make 4.

Press seams as desired. Make 4.

3. To a 5-unit section, sew 2 red 2½˝ squares. Press toward the squares. Make 2.

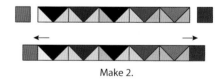

Make 2.

4. Arrange and sew 6 units together as shown. Press. Make 4.

Press seams as desired. Make 4.

5. To a 6-unit section, sew 2 light 2½" squares. Press toward the square. Make 2.

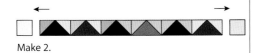
Make 2.

6. Sew 2 of the 5-unit sections to opposite sides of the Star section. Press as desired.

7. Sew the 5-unit/red square sections to the top and bottom of the Star section. Press as desired.

8. Sew the 6-unit sections to opposite sides of the Star section. Press as desired. Sew the 6-unit/light sections to the top and bottom of the Star section. Press.

Note

One set starts with and ends with gold. The other set starts with and ends with black.

LOOK-LIKE-BUT-AREN'T-FOUR-PATCHES BORDER

1. Sew 7 strips together in this order: gold, black, gold, black, gold, black, gold. Then sew 7 more strips together in this order: black, gold, black, gold, black, gold, black. Press as desired, and then cut each set of strips into 16 sections 2½" wide.

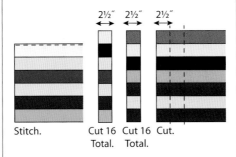
Stitch. Cut 16 Total. Cut 16 Total. Cut.

2. Refer to the Quilt Assembly Diagram, page 77. Arrange these sections around the quilt center to make sure black and gold fabrics alternate.

3. Sew 4 sections together. Press seams to the right. Make 4.

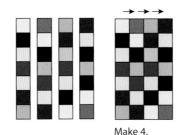
Make 4.

4. Sew 4 more sections together. Press seams toward the left. Make 4.

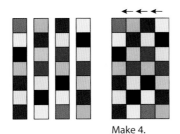
Make 4.

---

5. Sew 1 of each section together end-to-end to make a longer section. Press seam as desired. Make 4.

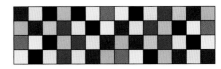
Make 4 total.

6. Sew blue strip to unit from Step 5. Press. Make 4.

CAKE STAND BASKET BLOCKS

For each block

SMALL HALF-SQUARE TRIANGLES

Mark the back of the 2½" light squares. Pair 1 light 2½" square to 1 red 2½" square. Sew on the diagonal line. Press. Square up the edge of the flipped light piece so it matches the red edge, if necessary, and then trim out the back 2 layers of fabric. Make 8.

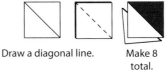
Draw a diagonal line.   Make 8 total.

LARGE HALF-SQUARE TRIANGLES

1. Pair 1 light 7" square with 1 red 7" square, right sides together. Refer to pages 7–8 for Half-Square triangle construction Steps 1–4.

2. Press the seam toward the medium fabric. Trim to 6½" × 6½". Each pair of squares yields 2 Half-Square triangles. You will use only 1 Half-Square triangle.

3. Arrange 8 small Half-Square triangles, 1 large Half-Square triangle, 2 red rectangles, and the 2 remaining red squares. Sew together in rows, and then sew the rows together. Press.

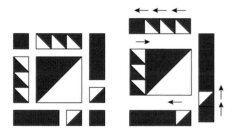

Make 4
total.

4. Repeat with the remaining red and light fabrics to make a total of 4 Basket blocks.

5. Sew 2 Look-Like-But-Aren't-Four-Patch border sections to the Star Section (blue border next to section). Press the seams toward the blue border.

6. Sew 2 Basket blocks to opposite ends of the Look-Like-But-Aren't-Four-Patches border sections. Note the placement of the blue border strip in relation to the Baskets. Press seams toward the Look-Like-But-Aren't-Four-Patches border sections. Sew this unit to the top and bottom of the Star section.

OUTSIDE BORDER

1. Draw a diagonal line on the wrong side of the light 4½″ square. Sew on the diagonal line, and flip the light square. Square up the blue piece if necessary, then trim out the back 2 layers.

Draw a diagonal line.

2. Repeat Step 1 to sew another light square to the unit. Press, square, and trim. Make 48.

Make 48
total.

3. Refer to the Quilt Assembly Diagram below for Steps 3–5. Arrange 12 units as shown to form 1 border for the quilt. Sew together in a row, and press seams as desired. Repeat to make 4 border rows.

4. Sew 2 border rows to the sides of the quilt top. Press seams toward the blue squares.

5. Sew 2 light squares to opposite ends of a remaining border row. Press seams toward the light squares. Make 2. Sew these border rows to the top and bottom of the quilt top. Press seams toward the blue squares.

6. Layer the top with batting and backing. Quilt and bind as desired.

Quilt Assembly Diagram

Untitled
by Merry Maricich.
Quilted by Wanda Rains.
66″ × 66″.

Snicker's Cake by Elizabeth Greenup. 56″ × 56″.

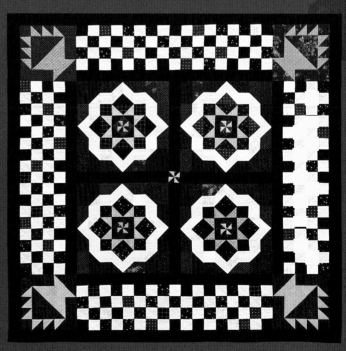

Have My Martha Cake and Eat It Too by Cate Franklin.
Quilted by Kaylen Reynolds. 57″ × 57″.

Martha Washington Cake

CAKE INGREDIENTS

- 1 cup butter
- 5 eggs, separated
- 1 cup sugar
- 1¼ cups flour
- 2 cups total dried apples, pears, apricots, cherries, and blueberries*

*Use more apples and pears than the other fruits.

- ¼ cup chopped or sliced almonds
- 1 teaspoon ground mace
- 1¼ teaspoons ground nutmeg
- 2 ounces (⅛ cup) orange juice

1. Preheat oven to 350°. Lightly grease and flour a 7″ × 11″ pan (small rectangular pan). If your pan is smaller or larger, you will adjust cooking time.

2. Allow eggs and butter to warm to room temperature.

3. Chop the fruits and nuts as follows: Dice apples, pears, and apricots. I used approximately ½ cup apples, ½ cup pears, then

⅓ cup each of apricots, cherries, and blueberries. Adjust quantities to your preference. Chop or slice almonds.

4. Separate egg whites from yolks. Set yolks aside.

5. Beat egg whites until soft peaks form. Cream the butter with a fork. Slowly add the butter to the egg whites. Slowly add the sugar to the egg whites and butter mixture. Add the egg yolks. Then slowly add the flour. Add mace, nutmeg, and orange juice.

6. By hand, stir in fruit and nuts.

7. Pour batter into pan and bake approximately 30 minutes (convection oven, longer with a nonconvection oven). Remember to adjust cooking time if your pan is a different size. When the cake is done, the top will be golden brown but not dark brown. Test cake with a toothpick for doneness. Toothpick should come out clean.

8. Frost cake when completely cool.

CREAM CHEESE FROSTING

- 6 ounces cream cheese, softened
- 2 tablespoons milk
- 2 teaspoons vanilla
- pinch of salt
- 4–5 cups powdered sugar

Blend the cream cheese, milk, vanilla, and salt. Gradually add the sugar, beating until frosting is smooth and of spreading consistency. If necessary, stir in additional milk, 1 tablespoon at a time.

two student *Challenges*

IT'S A MYSTERY CHALLENGE

The blocks for *It's a Mystery* are very easy, very quick (no triangles!), and very fun, and put together, the results are stunning (see my quilt on page 60)! After making my original *It's a Mystery* quilt, 13 students participated in a challenge with these blocks. They made 26 It's a Mystery blocks in their choice of colors and sent the blocks to me. I sorted them so that each student would receive 26 blocks—2 from each student plus 2 of their own—then sent the blocks back to the students. Using the blocks they received, students created their own quilts. The rules were that they had to use the blocks they received, but they didn't have to use all the blocks—or they could make more if they wanted to. Any setting was allowed. Here are the terrific results!

Beautiful Minds
by Mary Louise Washer.
Quilted by Barbara Dau.
72˝ × 72˝.

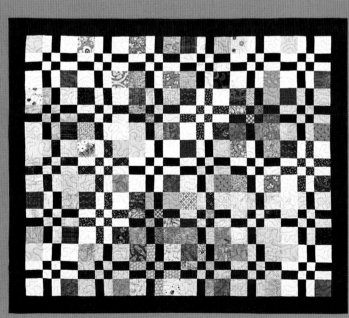

It's a Mystery Dessert Challenge
by Dorothy Finley.
Quilted by Sue Lohse.
58˝ × 50˝.

Mystery Dessert on the Prairie by Cate Franklin. Quilted by Carrie Peterson. 52″ × 52″.

Untitled by Merry Maricich. Quilted by Peggy Wilbur. 62″ × 69″.

Four by Four Friends by Suzanne Barsness. Quilted by Carrie Peterson. 49″ × 70″.

Mystery Challenge by Joseph Pepia. 68″ × 68″.

Moe's Choice by Joan Christ. Quilted by Carrie Peterson. 59″ × 59″.

THE LEMON CHIFFON QUILT CHALLENGE *Where it all began*

Lemon Chiffon One (below) was my very first dessert quilt, created in the summer of 2004. Since then, I have made over twenty dessert quilts! For this challenge, students chose their favorite dessert quilt and then created *Lemon Chiffon One* in that quilt's colors. I hope this challenge inspires you to choose your favorite *Sweet Treats* or *Patchwork Party, Delicious Desserts* quilt pattern, then choose your favorite color combination, and create a quilt that is uniquely your own. You really can make any quilt in any color combination you want!

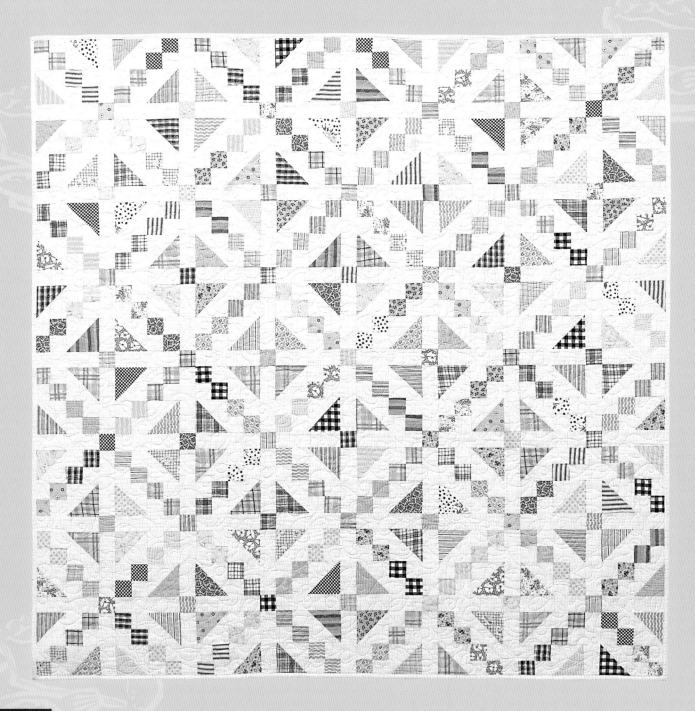

LEMON CHIFFON ONE in the colors of *Chocolate Decadence*

Fun Stuff by Mary Louise Washer. Quilted by Barbara Dau. 66″ × 81″.

LEMON CHIFFON ONE in the colors of *Apple Crisp*

Butterscotch Pudding by Ann Elizabeth Rindge. 53″ × 60″.

LEMON CHIFFON ONE in the colors of *Caramel Sundae*

Caramel Lemon Chiffon Sundae by Joseph Pepia. 59″ × 59″.

LEMON CHIFFON ONE in the colors of *Blueberry Cobbler*

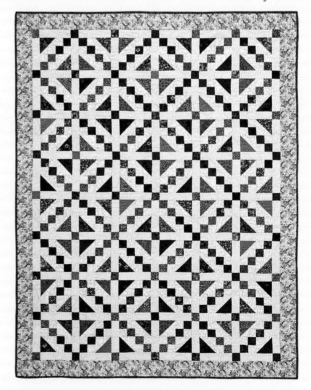

Blueberry Smoothie by Peggy Roebuck Jarrett. Quilted by Sue Lohse. 51″ × 65″.

LEMON CHIFFON ONE in the colors of *Pumpkin Pie*

Pumpkin Chiffon Pie by Joan Christ. Quilted by Carrie Peterson. 70″ × 70″.

LEMON CHIFFON ONE in the colors of *Key Lime Pie*

Antefriese Aperitif by Cheryl Nyberg. Quilted by Sue Lohse. 62″ × 49″.

LEMON CHIFFON ONE in the colors of *Hot Fudge Sundae*

Lemon Chiffon Challenge by Dorothy Finley. Quilted by Sue Lohse. 68″ × 61″.

LEMON CHIFFON ONE in the colors of *Triple Berry Tumble*

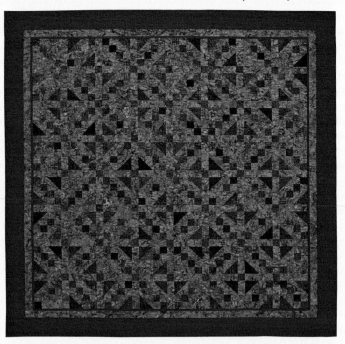

Untitled by Merry Maricich. Quilted by Peggy Wilbur. 69″ × 69″.

LEMON CHIFFON ONE
in the colors of *Lemon Blueberry Pound Cake*

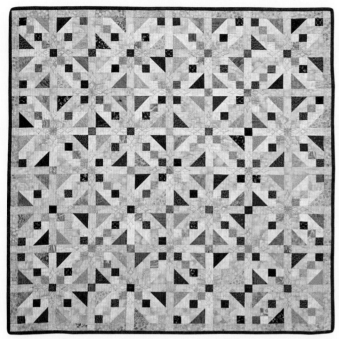

Lemon Chiffon Pound Cake with Blueberry Sauce by Linda L. Angel. 62″ × 62″.

LEMON CHIFFON ONE
in the colors of *Strawberry Shortcake and Chocolate Truffles*

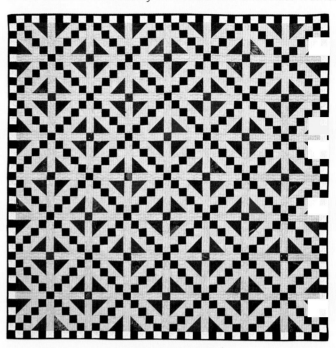

Strawberry Lemon Chiffon
by Suzanne Barsness. Quilted by Carrie Peterson. 69″ × 69″.

LEMON CHIFFON ONE
in the colors of *Almost Neapolitan*

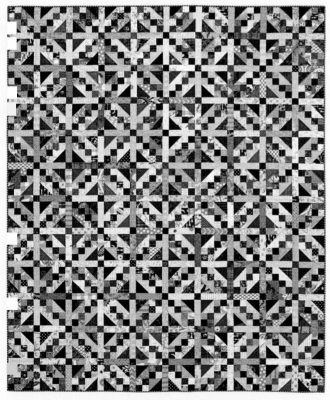

Chocolate Covered Strawberries
by Rachel Barsness. Quilted by Carrie Peterson. 70″ × 84″.

LEMON CHIFFON ONE
in the colors of *Pistachio Almond Cake*

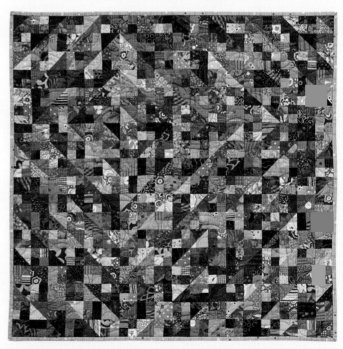

Spumoni by Rachel Barsness. Quilted by Carrie Peterson. 26″ × 26″.

LEMON CHIFFON ONE
in the colors of *Banana Split*

Mikey Likes It! by Cate Franklin. Quilted by Kaylen Reynolds. 70˝ × 70˝.

LEMON CHIFFON ONE
in the colors of *Valentine Cookies*

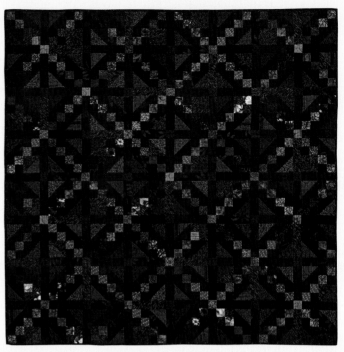

Wild Mountain Blackberry Pie
by Penny A. Hazelton. Quilted by Sue Lohse. 58˝ × 58˝.

LEMON CHIFFON ONE
in the colors of *Not Just Huckleberry Pie*

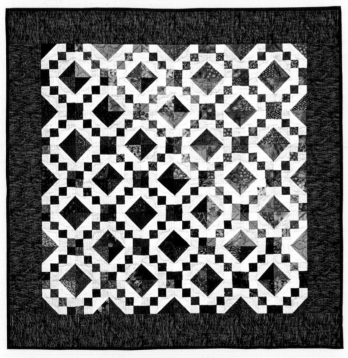

A Bit of Huckleberry Chiffon Pie
by Suzanne Barsness. Quilted by Carrie Peterson. 39˝ × 39˝.

LEMON CHIFFON ONE
in the colors of *Martha Washington Cake*

Little Martha by Joan Christ. Quilted by Carrie Peterson. 48˝ × 48˝.

About the Author

SANDY BONSIB is a teacher by profession and a quilter by passion. She has a graduate degree in education and has taught and lectured locally since 1993 and nationally since 1997. This is her ninth book (her second for C&T Publishing). She has appeared on *Lap Quilting* with Georgia Bonesteel, and *Simply Quilts* with Alex Anderson and was one of six featured artists on "Quilts of the Northwest," 1998. In 2003 she was nominated for teacher of the year. Sandy also coordinates Quilts for the Children, a group that has made over 3,000 quilts for the children of battered women. She mentors high school students doing their senior projects in quiltmaking. She also is a professional quilt appraiser.

Sandy lives on a small farm on Cougar Mountain in Issaquah, Washington, with her family and many animals. She also raises puppies for Guide Dogs for the Blind.

For information about Sandy's classes and lectures, visit her website at www.sandybonsib.com.

OTHER BOOKS BY SANDY BONSIB:

Great Titles *from* C&T PUBLISHING

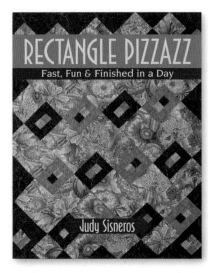

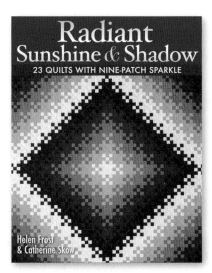

Available at your local retailer or **www.ctpub.com** *or* **800.284.1114**

For a list of other fine books from C&T Publishing,
ask for a free catalog:

C&T PUBLISHING, INC.
P.O. Box 1456
Lafayette, CA 94549
(800) 284-1114

Email: ctinfo@ctpub.com
Website: www.ctpub.com

C&T Publishing's professional photography services are now
available to the public. Visit us at www.ctmediaservices.com.

For quilting supplies:

COTTON PATCH
1025 Brown Ave.
Lafayette, CA 94549
Store: (925) 284-1177
Mail order: (925) 283-7883

Email: CottonPa@aol.com
Website: www.quiltusa.com

Note: Fabrics used in the quilts shown may not be
currently available, as fabric manufacturers keep most
fabrics in print for only a short time.

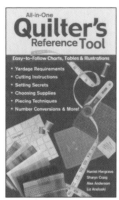

Mouth-Watering New Quilts & Desserts

- 10 pieced quilts with rich colors inspired by delicious desserts

- 10 finger-licking recipes to enjoy while you quilt

- Learn to use the color wheel to create rich color combinations

- Create a complex look with easy, basic blocks

Praise for Sandy's first book, *Sweet Treats*

"Cleverly tucked between four patch blocks, half-square triangles, and delicious desserts, is a detailed lesson on the importance of value and how it differs from color. Sandy lists the tools to help you choose values to make even the simplest patterns look stunning."

JOLI HINES SAYASANE, *Quilters Newsletter*

C&T PUBLISHING

10682
US $27.95
ISBN 978-1-57120-624-4
5279

9 781571 206244